HG

D1250935

INFANTS WITHOUT FAMILIES

INFANTS WITHOUT FAMILIES

The Case For and Against
Residential Nurseries

by

ANNA FREUD

and

DOROTHY BURLINGHAM

223425

INTERNATIONAL UNIVERSITIES PRESS, INC.
New York   New York

CONTENTS

CHAP.   PAGE

FOREWORD 7

FOUR ASPECTS OF DEVELOPMENT
    BETWEEN BIRTH AND TWO YEARS.... 11
    MUSCULAR CONTROL
    SPEECH DEVELOPMENT
    HABIT TRAINING
    FEEDING

EARLY RELATIONS BETWEEN
    RESIDENTIAL INFANTS 27
    OTHER CHILDREN TREATED LIKE TOYS, ETC.
    OTHER CHILDREN TREATED AS A DISTURBANCE, ETC.
    OTHER CHILDREN TREATED AS A MENACE, ETC.
    OTHER CHILDREN COMFORTED, SOOTHED, ETC.
    INFANTS HELPING EACH OTHER
    DIRECT EDUCATONAL INFLUENCE ON EACH OTHER
    FRIENDSHIP BETWEEN INFANTS
    INSTANCES OF LOVE-PLAY, ETC.

INTRODUCTION OF THE MOTHER - RELA-
    TIONSHIP INTO NURSERY-LIFE 53
    FORMATION OF ARTIFICIAL FAMILIES
    SPECIFIC NATURE AND CONSEQUENCES OF THE
        MOTHER-RELATIONSHIP
    FURTHER CONSEQUENCES, ETC.
    SPONTANEOUS ATTACHMENTS TO A GROWN-UP

CHAP.   PAGE

SOME ASPECTS OF INSTINCTUAL SATIS-
FACTION AND FRUSTRATION IN FAM-
ILY- AND NURSERY-LIFE 65

BODILY INTIMACY BETWEEN INFANT AND MOTHER
AUTO-EROTIC HARITS IN A RESIDENTEIAL NURSERY
THE SMALL CHILD'S WISH TO BE ADMIRED
  (INFANTILE EXHIBITIONISM)
INFANTILE CURIOSITY
SUMMARY

THE ROLE OF THE FATHER IN THE RESI-
DENTIAL NURSERY 101

RELATIONSHIP TO DEAD FATHERS
RELATIONSHIP TO ABSENT FATHERS
HISTORY OF A PHANTASY-FATHER

THE GROWTH OF THE CHILD'S PERSONAL-
ITY UNDER NURSERY CONDITIONS .. 117

IMITATION IN THE NURSERY
  A. IMITATION OF GROWN-UPS
  B. IMITATION OF CONTRASTING BEHAVIOT
    PATTERNS
  C. OTHER MODELS OF IMITATION
FAMILY BEHAVIOR PATTERNS IN THE NURSERY
  A. MOTHER-CHILD PLAY OF MOTHERLESS
    CHILDREN
  B. ADOPTION OF MASCULINE ATTITUDES BY BOYS
    WHO LIVE WITHOUT FATHERS
  C. QUICK ADOPTION OF THE EMOTIONAL ATTI-
    TUDES OF THE FAMILY CIRCLE
DEVELOPMENT THROUGH IDENTIFICATION.
CHARACTER FORMATION

CONCLUSIONS 127

FOREWORD

THE observations recorded in this publication have been collected during practical educational work in the three houses of the Hampstead Nursery:

13, Wedderburn Road, London, N. W. 3 (Nursery-School);

5, Netherhall Gardens, London, N. W. 3 (50 resident children from birth to 5 years);

"New Barn," Lindsell near Dunmow, Essex (40 resident children from 2 to 10 years).

The Hampstead Nursery is a Colony of the Foster Parents' Plan for War Children, Inc., New York, and as such owes its whole existence to American generosity. Like the other Colonies of the Foster Parents' Plan it provides wartime homes for children whose family life has been broken up temporarily or permanently owing to war conditions. Like the other Colonies of the Foster Parents' Plan, although residential it is not run on institutional lines. It tries to re-establish for the children what they have lost: the security of a stable home with its opportunities for individual development. The only characteristic of "institutional" life which it is powerless to avoid is the absence of the family itself.

War conditions, i.e. the fathers' service in the Forces, full-time factory work of many mothers, evacuation as a precautionary measure and the destruction of many small homes through bombing have disrupted family life among large sections of the population. Consequently many infants, though not parentless, were rendered homeless. They had to be collected in residential nurseries and there suffered the experience of "life without the family" which is, in peace-time, reserved for the inhabitants of orphanages. The effect, not merely of the shock of being separated from the family, but of the lack of continuous emotional contact between the infant and his parents with the consequent absence of the specific formative influence inherent in the family tie, was thus open to view in many more cases than usual and seemed to us worthy of study and description.

It is not at present possible to predict how many of the children, now in residential nurseries, will be found to be permanently homeless when the war is ended. A preliminary survey of our own children's circumstances has shown that, present conditions remaining unaltered, 59 per cent could return to their families as soon as their fathers are demobilized and their mothers stop war-work. 41 per cent would remain homeless for various reasons: because they are illegitimate and their mothers, as unskilled or domestic workers, unable to maintain a home; because their families are destitute and either morally or financially unable to take care of them; because their mothers have lost touch with them during the war and cannot be traced; because their mothers are ill, either in tuberculosis hospitals or in mental homes; because their mothers have died during the war so that a return home depends on eventual re-marriage of the father; because they have lost both parents in the raids.

Possibly this percentage of homeless children is considerably higher in the Hampstead Nursery where this investigation was carried out than in the official residential nurseries. It is possible, too, that post-war efforts will be directed towards dealing with homelessness without the help of residential institutions, i.e. by means of legal adoptions, official billeting schemes, etc. However this may be, homeless children will doubtless be numerous and will present a problem. Our attempt to evaluate the advantages and disadvantages of residential (institutional) life at different phases and in different aspects of the infants' development may furnish some material to help towards the solution of this problem.

DOROTHY BURLINGHAM.   ANNA FREUD.

The contents of this book have been included in the Reports of the Nursery, sent each month to the Foster Parsents' Plan for War Children in New York. The development and aims of the Hampstead Nursery have been set out in detail in a former publication by the same authors, *War and Children,* International University Press, 1944, New York, N. Y.

FOUR ASPECTS OF DEVELOPMENT BETWEEN
BIRTH AND TWO YEARS

IT is recognized among workers in education and in child
psychology that children who have spent their entire lives
in institutions present a type of their own and differ in
various respects from children who develop under the conditions of family life. Knowledge about the nature of these
differences has been gained partly through individual observation where such institutional children have in later life
turned anti-social or criminal [see Aichhorn, *Wayward
Youth*], partly through group observation of large numbers
of children evacuated as babies to residential nurseries
during this war. Superficial observation of children of this
kind leaves a conflicting picture. They resemble, so far as
outward appearances are concerned, children of middle-
class families: they are well developed physically, properly
nourished, decently dressed, have acquired clean habits and
decent table manners, and can adapt themselves to rules and
regulations. So far as character development is concerned,
they often prove—to everybody's despair and despite many
efforts—not far above the standard of destitute or neglected
children. This shows up especially after they have left the
institutions.

It is because of these failures of development that in recent
years thoughtful educationists have more and more turned
against the whole idea of residential nurseries as such, and
have devised methods of boarding out orphaned or destitute

children with foster families, (etc.). But since all efforts of this kind will probably not be able to do away altogether with the need for residential homes for infants, it remains a question of interest how far failures of the kind described are inherent in the nature of such institutions as distinct from family life, and how far they could be obviated if the former were ready and able to change their methods.

Careful comparison of our own residential children with children of the same ages who live with their own families has taught us some interesting facts. Advantages and disadvantages vary to an astonishing degree according to the periods of development.

BIRTH TO FIVE MONTHS

Babies between birth and about five months of age, when not breast-fed under either condition, develop better in our nursery than in the average proletarian household. Their gain in weight is more regular and intestinal disturbances are less frequent; their skin, colouring and general appearance are more satisfactory. In times of illness the absence of the tension and anxiety which the young mother invariably feels is certainly of advantage to the child. Mothers who reared their first children in their own homes and now have a third or fourth baby with us are usually full of praise when they compare the progress of this "institutional" child with their first "family" ones. The reasons are not difficult to find: more carefully prepared food, with variation in the food formulas whenever necessary; plenty of air in outdoor life, whenever the weather permits; less economy in laundry; skilled and regular handling and removal from the disturbances of a proletarian household in restricted quarters.

Breast-fed babies are, of course, better off than bottle-fed babies wherever they are. Our best results are found in babies who are breast-fed by their own mothers in our home. They show the double advantage of mother's care combined with the careful hygiene of the nursery.

FIVE TO TWELVE MONTHS

In the second half of the first year the picture changes definitely to our disadvantage. Whenever we have an opportunity to compare our five to twelve-months-old babies with family babies out of average homes we are struck by the greater liveliness and better social response of the family child. The latter is usually more advanced in reaching out for objects and in active play. He is more active in watching the movements of people in the room and more responsive to their leaving or entering, since whoever comes and goes is known to him and concerns him in some way. A child of that age is, of course, unable to take in and differentiate between all the changing personalities in a baby ward or big nursery. For the same reason the baby's emotional response to changing expression, face or voice, of the grown-up person may be slower to develop. His ability to imitate which he develops from the eighth month onward is stimulated in a lesser degree where contact with the grown-up is less frequent, or less close, or has to be divided between several grown-ups as is inevitable in a nursery. Even where our residential babies are stronger and healthier, these differences in intellectual and emotional development are sufficient to make the private baby appear more "advanced" and therefore more satisfactory. The comparative backwardness of the residential baby at this stage is due to the comparative unfulfilment of his emotional needs which at this age equal in importance the various needs of the body. The relationship to the mother of the small newborn infant was based on the gratification of bodily needs. Emotional interplay between child and grown-up occurred exclusively during feeding, bathing and changing, and was therefore no less frequent under nursery conditions than in the home. Between five-twelve months emotional interplay and the intellectual stimulation which results from it, is more or less distributed over all the waking hours of the child's day. Consequently, the nursery child, who receives individual attention only when fed, bathed or changed, is at a disadvantage. The amount of further individual attention — play hour, outings in pram, baby gymnastics, etc. — which can be given to a child depends on the staffing of the nursery and other routine arrangements. Attention of this kind has of course to be given by a mother-substitute to whom the child is attached and is valueless when offered by visitors, strangers or occasional "voluntary workers".

On the whole we may say that in the second half of the residential child's first year the loss in emotional satisfaction outweighs the gain in bodliy care.

ONE TO TWO YEARS OF AGE

1. MUSCULAR CONTROL.

With the beginning of the second year the scales turn again in our favor. The great event in the child's life is his new ability to move freely and to control his movements, an ability which progresses quickly from crawling to walking, running, climbing, jumping, and is continued with the handling and moving of objects, as pushing, pulling, dragging, carrying, etc. Even where mothers fully recognize what intense pleasure the child derives from exercising these new functions, they are, because of outward circumstances, usually unable to give the child free play and thus further his development in this respect. There is in the ordinary household no space for the child to move in or no safety when he moves in the given space. Most mothers are only too well aware of the dangers from fires, boiling water, falls from heights or injury from furniture or falling objects which the child might pull down on himself. The result is that toddlers in their own homes remain in their cribs, or strapped to a pram, or at best confined to the narrow space of a playpen, at a period when in a nursery like ours they cover miles in continual movement about their room. Some children at this period for a while disregard all toys and show little interest in their companions; they behave as if they were drunk with the idea of space and even of speed; they crawl, walk, march and run, and revert from one method of locomotion to the other with the greatest pleasure. These children mostly use toys where they can include them in the continual game of moving. Chairs and pots are not used to sit on but are propelled about the room. Soft toys and animals on wheels are "taken for walks", balls are followed, and some children, after they have once gained an easy balance, show special pleasure in moving a toy along in each hand while they move themselves. Sometimes for an hour on end the whole population of the Junior Toddler room is on the move, circling around, crossing and recrossing like people on a skating rink.

Handling, of course, is not confined to toys. Whatever is loose in the room (whether coal bucket, nappy-bins, pail, broom, etc.) is included in the interest and is handled and explored. If permitted, the children use to the full the newly-developed functions of opening, undoing, pulling out and especially unscrewing. It is easy to imagine that actions of this nature which, when several children are together, resemble those of a demolition squad, cannot be tolerated without damage and expense in a private household. It is not only the child whom the mother wants to safeguard from the objects, but similarly the objects which she has to safeguard from the child.

Freedom to use hands and legs in the way described has further advantages besides the intense pleasure and satisfaction which the child gains by exercising them. Handling quickly becomes more and more skilful under these conditions, so that the toddler of about 18 months of age can already help to set out tables and chairs for his own meal, feed himself, help at dressing or undressing himself and generally co-operates actively in whatever happens, at an age when private children are often still fed on the mother's lap and handled as if they were passive objects. These differences in activity and earlier control of movement through exercise and opportunity create the appearance of enormous precocity of development of the nursery child.

2. SPEECH DEVELOPMENT.

But it would be a serious mistake to overestimate the advantages gained in this field and not to correlate them with retardations and disadvantages which occur at the same time in other spheres of the child's life. The achievement of muscular control is only one of the tasks reserved for the second year of life. An equally important one is the development of speech. Observations within academic psychology have established the fact that at one year the average vocabulary of a child is two words, and that at two years it may be any number of words from 40 to more than 1,200 with a wide variety of phrases and sentences. Whenever we compare our nursery children over one year with private children in this respect we find that they compare unfavorably. The disparity in development does not start as early as the baby stage in talking. Many observations in our baby-room prove that our children under one year "speak", that is babble and chatter gibberish, extensively and certainly not less than other children. Some babies are, of course, more proficient than others in this respect.

The greatest talker of the baby-room was a girl who, at the age of 9 to 10 months, had developed great ability in producing a variety of sounds. At that time she showed little interest in the usual baby toys, but talked to herself nearly all day long. With her it was easy to distinguish between the various sounds and tones which seemed exciting in themselves: rrda, grra, irrga, daraa, dada, ida, and others, sing-songs or melodies, which served to call certain people.

Her pleasure in talking and her rising excitement while doing so were especially apparent.

But even though most of our babies possess the required two words at one year, speech development becomes slower and slower from then on. The good start made in babyhood is not continued in the same manner. When tested, at the age of two, for instance, even those of our children who are well up to standard and forward in other respects, show some six months' retardation of speech.

The retardation in the second year may be due to two reasons. The first is that the child at home is the only non-speaking member of a community in which speech is the method of communication. In the nursery, where the junior toddler group is usually divided off from older children, the child lives in a community of non-talking playmates where speech would not be of immediate help to him. If speech is learned largely by imitation, then the opportunity to learn is certainly restricted. The second reason is probably more important still. Though imitation of elder brothers and sisters plays a great part, especially in extending the vocabulary, the beginning of real speech develops on the basis of close contact between child and parents. The child has instinctive understanding of whatever emotion moves the mother; he watches her face and through imitation reproduces her facial expressions. It is the same emotional interplay with the resulting imitation which is a powerful drive towards expression in speech. With the restriction of this interplay in the absence of the mother there is a definite lessening in the urge to speak.

Some children develop a separate language or sequence of sounds to be used exclusively for contact with their mother. This was apparent with one of our baby girls of nine months, for instance, whose mother worked in the household of the nursery and naturally appeared in the babyroom at all hours of the day. The child began to produce a special tone to greet her which sounded like the clucking of ducks. In the course of a month this sound had become completely different from all her other sound productions so that everybody knew from afar when her mother had entered the room. At eleven months the same baby went through a stage of dissatisfaction in which she found it especially intolerable to have wishes postponed or denied. She always wanted her mother to pick her up out of her cot as quickly as possible. At this time she stopped producing the pleasant clucking sound at sight of her mother and adopted a grumble which she kept up each time until the mother had fulfilled her wish. The substitution of the grumbling for the happy clucking sound designated a change in the relationship to the mother from satisfaction and acceptance to impatient demandingness.

Inquiries in other residential nurseries have confirmed the impresion gained in our own. When children are home on visits, for instance at Christmas or during their mothers' holidays, they sometimes gain in speech in one or two weeks what they would have taken three months to gain in the nursery. Similarly there are many examples of children brought up at home who lose their newly acquired ability to speak during an absence of the mother. Regression of this kind is further proof of the inter-relation between contact with the mother and learning to speak.

This difference of progress in the two stages illustrates the fact that two different factors are at work in speech development: one is the simple pleasure in the production of sound, a pleasure which is partly centred in the mouth itself and partly aroused by the volume and quantity of tone and sound production, rhythm, etc., a pleasure comparable to other early gratifications of the self-regarding or so-called "auto-erotic" kind. The other factor is an urge towards expression and communication with the loved people of the outside world; the pleasure gained by its fulfilment might be called other-regarding or pleasure based on object-relationship. The examples above show both factors at work side by side in an instructive way.

This differentiation explains why speech development progresses normally in the first year and is delayed in the second year under residential conditions. The first factor, i.e. the urge to gain oral auto-erotic pleasure, is present in full force. Like all auto-erotic gratifications of this age (sucking, rhythmic movements, masturbation) it is all the more active, the more the child is left to itself. Speech development progresses on this basis, but only to the limits of baby-talk. The second factor, i.e. communication and imitation on the basis of the relationship to the mother, is less active where a mother is not present; hence the difficulty and retardation at the time when this second factor should supersede the first one in importance. One or two years later these differences are cancelled out again; the child is then a full member of a group and speech has become independent of the mother-child relationship.

The differences in speech development described here do not apply to children who enter a residential nursery only after they have learned to speak, that is, it is not a difference in the use but in the development of the function of speech.

3. HABIT TRAINING.

The third important task to be achieved or at least partially achieved during the child's second year is habit training. Here again the residential child is at a disadvantage. It is easier within the routine of a nursery than under the pressure of work in an ordinary household to be clean, orderly, punctual and hygienic about habit training; but wherever forcible methods are not used, the results of habit training are slow to come under residential conditions. In this sphere imitation, the fact that the child lives in a group of other children of the same age who are all equally dirty, can be discounted as an agent. Habit training is not learnt by imitation. What makes itself felt is the fact that habit training, if not achieved in babyhood as a pure reflex action, is the result of a restriction which the child imposes on important inner urges under the influence of the mother. If the child is attached to and handled by one person exclusively, as happens at home, this restriction will develop in consequence of his emotional dependence. Whenever the child changes hands, or is cared for by varying nurses, as happens invariably in a nursery, or does not care for the nurses who handle him, the process will be lengthened and made more difficult. It has been shown up at the time of mass evacuation how young children who have been perfectly clean at home, lose their bladder and sphincter control when separated from their mothers. It is a known fact in all residential nurseries that a child whose training for cleanliness presents special difficulties can finally be made clean only if taken over completely by one person for a while. It is equally well known that many children in nurseries maintain their good habits only when in contact with certain nurses and will refuse to function when helped by others. These differences in personal contact are far more important for the final result than any other factors — observing regular times, regulation of diet, etc. Habit training can, of course, be achieved under pressure of fear and punishment even where emotional contact of a positive kind is absent. But no conscientious and understanding educator will ever advocate such methods.

The child's muscular skill and independence, gained in the nursery as described above, plays no part in the development of cleanliness.

4. FEEDING.

The position is again completely different where eating is concerned. There is a marked difference between the child's reaction to food under home and residential conditions, but on this point the advantages are on the side of the residential child, or at least they may be so if the institutional setting is favorable. This means that in most residential nurseries the children are "good eaters", i.e. are interested in their food and enjoy it if it is good, and that eating difficulties are on the whole less prevalent than in private homes. Where abnormal reactions occur, they appear rather in the form of greed and over-eating than in the form of inhibition, lack of appetite or refusal of food. The popular explanation of this well-known fact is that children in their own homes are frequently "spoilt" in this respect, that is that many mothers, at least in middle-class families, are over-anxious where feeding is concerned, and that in some cases they urge the child to eat and even to over-eat. These children then refuse what is offered to them, develop idiosyncracies, etc. It is taken as proof of the correctness of this explanation that such eating-difficulties do not develop in families where mothers are careless, negligent and not interested in the feeding of the child. It would thus seem that the child eats all the better the less the mother worries about the matter.

This theory, though only superficial and incomplete, is still correct in one main point: namely, that eating difficulties are closely connected with the child's relationship to the mother. When followed up from the first stages of the breast-or bottle-feeding of the newborn baby, this interrelation of reaction to the mother and reaction to food may be described as follows:

Interest in food begins earlier than interest in people. In the first weeks of life the newborn baby experiences nearly everything that reaches him from the external world as unpleasant. He is still used to the lack of stimuli in the intra-uterine existence. Light, noise, change of temperature are all equally unpleasant and even frightening. The first pleasant experience is the intake of milk, that is of food which satisfies the urge of hunger. With the constant repetition of these pleasant experiences, the child slowly learns to recognize that at least part of the outside world is pleasurable. He forms an attachment to food — milk — and, developing further from this point, to the person who feeds him. As described before, love for the food becomes the basis of love for the mother.

The emotional attachment of the child to the mother, to the father and to the other people of his immediate surroundings later on outgrows the stage where material gain — satisfaction of hunger — or gain of pleasure generally are the only important factors. In the course of childhood material love of this kind changes to real love, which takes into account the qualities and individuality of a loved person, and is able to give and even to make sacrifices in exchange for what is received.

But the experiences of the first year, when love for the food and love for a mother were identical, leave their imprint on the reaction to food throughout life. The child from his side shows every inclination to treat food given by the mother as he treats the mother, which means that all the possible disturbances of the child-mother relationship turn easily into eating disturbances. When we observe cases of "bad eaters" it becomes clear how exactingness towards the mother can turn to greed, obstinacy against the mother to a tightly closed mouth and refusal of food, and anger with the mother to playing with or wasting of food. These, of course, are not the only known reasons for eating difficulties in childhood, but they are the most primitive and most common ones.

Wherever the mother in her own behaviour perpetuates the feeding circumstances of the first year (i.e. wherever she insists on giving the food actively, on urging the child to eat it for her sake, where she is angry, disappointed or offended when the food remains uneaten, as if it were a personal affront to her), she strengthens the child's infantile attitudes to eating and makes it impossible for him to outgrow them. The inclinations of mother and child then work in the same direction and the child continues as in babyhood to treat the food as he treats the mother and the mother as he treats the food.

Wherever the mother adapts her behaviour to the growing abilities of the child, where she recedes into the background as the giver of the food and only provides food in a more distant and unemotional manner, the child will enter into a next stage of reaction to food: he will eat, or refuse nourishment, according to whether he is hungry or not, and not according to whether he loves or rejects his mother, or wants to please or anger her. Even though the basic significance of food will remain the same for the individual's unconscious, and may show up in times of emotional strain or mental illness, so far as the child's conscious and normal life is concerned, eating will be enabled to follow the dictates of hunger, and will be less drawn into the complications of the child's affections; that means the child will become a "good eater".

We can now understand why it is that the conscientious and anxious mothers produce eating difficulties, whereas the negligent mothers have children who eat well.

Under institutional conditions the absence of the mother, which is a serious drawback in so many ways, proves in this respect for once an advantage. There are certainly institutional children who eat too much for emotional reasons: they try to substitute the satisfaction of one instinctual urge — hunger — for the satisfaction of another — love. But on the whole, in an institution feeding is a matter of eating as such, without the idea of a mother figure interpolated between the child and the food. Food is liked for its own sake, and eating is one of the recognized pleasures of all institutional life.

The pleasure can, of course, be spoiled or lessened if it is surrounded with too much discipline, as, for instance, long waiting, which at this age is an excessive strain; sitting quiet, which is never again so difficult as in the toddler stage; insistence on table manners, i. e. use of the spoon before use of an instrument comes naturally; insistence on eating everything and on "eating up". The pleasure in eating can on the other hand be greatly strengthened if the child is allowed some freedom of movement, some freedom of choice regarding type and quantity of food, and if manners are not considered important in themselves but allowed to develop as a natural result of growing skill. It is for purely practical reasons easier to give the child this freedom in a nursery than in a family.

Since the child in a nursery never eats alone, mealtimes, with the pleasure they bring, can be made to play an important part in the child's development towards taking pleasure in social life, and adaptation to it.

SUMMARY.

To sum up: The institutional child in the first two years has advantages in all those spheres of his life which are independent of the emotional side of his nature; he is at a disadvantage wherever the emotional tie to the mother or to the family is the mainspring of development. Comparisons between children under these contrasting conditions serve to show that certain achievements such as speech and habit training are closely related to the child's emotions, even though this may not be apparent at first glance.

EARLY RELATIONS BETWEEN RESIDENTIAL
INFANTS

WE have chosen four different aspects of the infant's life
to illustrate the differences in development under home and
institutional conditions: Muscular Control, Speech Development, Habit Training and Feeding. The differences in each
case were quantitative: muscular control and good eating
habits develop more quickly and easily in institutions, speech
and habit training are delayed when the mother's influence
is missing. Still, all children will eventually walk and talk,
be trained for cleanliness and become more or less independent eaters. Development is helped or hindered by the
outside setting, early acquired disturbances may leave their
traces for all later life, but essentially the lines of development will remain the same.

This is not so where the child's emotional life is concerned. Here, change of condition, i.e. lack of the family
setting, produces serious qualitative changes. The basic
emotional needs of the institutional child are, of course,
the same as those of the child who lives at home. But these
needs meet with a very different fate. One important instinctual need, that for early attachment to the mother,
remains as we know more or less unsatisfied; consequently
it may become blunted, which means that the child after
a while ceases to search for a mother substitute and fails
to develop all the more highly organized forms of love
which should be modelled on this first pattern. Or, the

dissatisfaction may have the opposite effect: the dissatisfied and disappointed child may overstress his desire to find a mother, and remain continually on the look-out for new mother figures whose affection he might gain. These are the infants who change their allegiances all the time, are always ready to attach themselves to the latest newcomer, and are at the same time exacting, demanding, apparently passionate, but always disappointed in whatever new attachment they form.

On the other hand, another form of emotional contact, that with other children, is precociously stimulated and developed. Under normal family conditions contact with other children develops only after the child-mother relationship has been firmly established. Brothers and sisters are taken into account for ulterior motives: for instance, as playmates and helpmates. But apart from these relations with them, love and hate towards them are usually not developed directly, but by way of the common relation to the parents. So far as they are rivals for the parents' love, they arouse jealousy and hate; so far as they are under the parents' protection and therefore "belong", they are tolerated, and even loved. Under institutional conditions the matter is completely different. At the time when the infant lacks opportunities to develop attachment to a stable mother figure, he is overwhelmed with opportunities to make contact with playmates of the same age. Whereas the grown-ups in his life come and go in a manner which inevitably bewilders the child, these playmates are more or less constant and important figures in his world.

Matters in this way are completely reversed. These institutional children do not start out to meet a world of contemporaries, secure in the feeling that they are firmly attached to one "mother person" to whom they can revert. They live in an "age group" that is, in a dangerous world, peopled by individuals who are as unsocial and as unrestrained as they are themselves. In a family they would, at the age of 18 months, be the "little ones" whom the elder brothers and sisters are ready to protect and consider. In a crowd of other toddlers they have to learn unduly early to defend themselves and their property, to stand up for their own rights, and even to consider the rights of others. This means that they have to become social at an age when it is normal to be asocial. Under pressure of these circumstances they develop a surprising range of reactions: love, hate, jealousy, rivalry, competition, protectiveness, pity, generosity, sympathy and even understanding.

In the following pages we illustrate this point with occurrences from the daily life of our own residential children between one, two or three years old. The examples range from instances where playmates are treated as if they were dolls or lifeless objects, to occasions where the relations between the children seem hardly different from those between adults.

OTHER CHILDREN TREATED LIKE TOYS OR LIFELESS OBJECTS. INDIFFERENCE TOWARDS THEIR FEELINGS.

Little or no illustration is needed for the fact that normally infants have little conception of other infants' feelings, and only take notice of their presence when that can be made use of for the purposes of play. The other child then serves the purpose of a doll or teddy bear, with the one disadvantage that this living toy is not so accommodating as the lifeless ones. This behavior is not restricted to very early stages of development, but occurs quite frequently around the second year, especially at times when the infant copies a motherly grown-up in his imaginative play.

 1. Rose, 20 months, looked on with interest when several children had their noses wiped. Suddenly she picked up an old envelope, ran from one child to the other, and wiped their noses with it.

The action was imitative and expressed her phantasy of being the nurse; but no feeling for the children was included in it.

 2. Paul, two years, loved to comb the other children's hair, disregarding the fact that they disliked it. He rushed from one child to another and maltreated their hair with a comb. There was only one child who did not mind, Larry, twenty months. Thus, whenever Paul had made a child cry with his combing, he ran back and combed Larry, before he attacked his next unwilling victim. This game continued sometimes for several minutes.

In this instance, as in Example 1, all the pleasure lies in the action of combing, and feelings for the other children play no part.

 3. Freda, twenty months, pushed four children over in succession and tried to sit and rock on them. Each of them cried in turn and had to be rescued from her. When Freda was defeated in her aims, she collected five soft toys, piled them up and rocked on them.

In this case it is difficult to decide whether the toys were substitutes for the children or the children, in her first attempt, for toys. It is more likely that both, children and toys, were substitutes for some other imaginary partner in Freda's phantasy.

The same type of behavior can constantly be observed where feeding is concerned. Children start to feed each other very early, the pleasure evidently being derived from the fact that they carry out actively what at other times they submit to. This must not be mistaken for a wish to satisfy the other child's appetite, which would be a purely altruistic gesture.

4. Rose, twenty-one months, asked urgently "more, more," when she had finished her first helping. The nurse who was feeding Christopher, sixteen months, next to Rose, left the table to fetch Rose's second helping. Rose immediately picked up the spoon and continued to feed Christopher.

5. Stella, eighteen months, was sitting next to Agnes, fifteen months. She took Agnes' spoon and tried to feed her. She heaped up a spoonful of food and put it into her own mouth, then she pushed an empty spoon into Agnes' mouth. This she repeated several times until finally she emptied the whole contents of Agnes' plate into her own.

In this case it is easy to see that the action which apparently takes the other child into account is in reality purely egoistic. The pleasure of feeding — active repetition of passive experience, imaginative play — is added to the pleasure of eating.

OTHER CHILDREN TREATED MERELY AS A DISTURBANCE. AGGRESSIVE ACTS AGAINST THEM.

There are three sets of circumstances which give occasion for aggressive reactions of one infant towards another. One is the indifference and lack of realization that the other child is an equally sensitive human being, which has already been described. The other two comprise instances when the other child is felt to be a hindrance in the way of fulfilling a desire, i.e. when the playmate either claims the love or attention of a grown-up person whom the infant wants to have exclusively to himself — jealousy, examples 6 and 7 — or when the playmate claims a toy which the child has no intention of surrendering — envy, examples 8, 9 and 10.

6. Freda, eighteen months, and Violet, thirteen months, were both playing on the floor. Violet asked to sit on the nurse's lap and was taken up. So Freda, too, wanted to sit on the nurse's lap. She hit Violet until she, too, was taken on the lap; at first she was nice to Violet but soon turned against her and began to hit her hard.

7. Agnes, nineteen months, sat on the nurse's lap; Edith, sixteen months, tried to push her off but was not successful. Edith hit Agnes; Agnes pulled Edith's hair; Edith pulled Agnes' hair. The nurse moved Agnes to her other side to protect her against Edith, who was the stronger one. Edith suddenly thwarted, looked at the nurse with fury, hit her, pulled her hair and then suddenly petted her and gave her a kiss.

8. Agnes, nineteen months, had a teddy bear in her arms, Paul, two years, rushed to her, grabbed the teddy and ran away with it. Agnes screamed and pursued Paul. At first he ran faster than she, then she reached him, got hold of his arm and ran with him through the nursery, both children screaming. Agnes fell, and as she still clung to Paul's arms, he fell too. On the floor, she grabbed hold of his hair and pulled it. He bit her arm; she pinched his cheek; he hit her and, in doing so, lost the teddy. Agnes took it quickly, got up and ran away, hiding behind the nurse's apron.

9. Rose, twenty-two months, had a wooden horse for pushing, but did not show much interest in it. Sam, twenty months, was delighted with it and pushed it across the room. After a while Rose ran up to him silently and took the horse. Sam looked up amazed and began to cry. Rose passed him by with the horse. He got up his courage, walked after her and grabbed hold of her dress. Rose fell down, but still held the horse. Sam now pulled at one end of the horse, Rose at the other, both screaming. Sam after all captured the horse and pushed off, still crying. Rose ran after him, and, with a quick movement, recaptured the horse. Sam threw himself on the floor in despair, and Rose, who pushed her horse along, happened to trip over him and fell. This restarted the fight, both pulled hard at the horse, both cried, both refused to take another toy. In the end the nurse removed the horse and peace reigned immediately.

10. Terry, two years two months, loved the big push-dog of the nursery, and all other children somehow accepted the assumption that he had the first right to play with it. When he was away at home for 2½ days, Agnes, nineteen months, got a chance to play with the dog. When Terry returned he wanted to resume ownership, but Agnes did not feel inclined to surrender the dog. Terry pulled and shook the dog; Agnes screamed but held tight. Terry threw the dog over and Agnes went down with it. She clung to it with one hand and grabbed hold of Terry's leg with the other. Terry scratched Agnes. Agnes got up, still holding on to the dog and pulled Terry's hair. Terry hit her and Agnes continued steadily to pull his hair, still holding on to the dog with one hand. When Terry again pushed Agnes and the dog

over, the nurse rescued her and Agnes only wanted to be comforted and gave up interest in the dog.

Whenever envy and jealousy arise between the children, this results in outbreaks of aggression of considerable force. The methods of aggression vary according to the stage of development reached: biting, hair-pulling, hammering on the head, hitting, pushing over take first place between the age of fifteen and twenty-four months. Throwing things and spitting only occur with certain types of children, and more frequently after than before the third year (examples 11 and 12).

11. Christopher, thirteen months, bit Charlie, his twin brother, several times, pulled his hair constantly; hit Babette, eleven months. Christopher, fourteen months, knocked with a brick on Charlie's head; bit Sophie, fourteen months. Charlie, fourteen months, bit Christopher.

12. Freda, twenty-one months, wanted to precede Edith, twenty-two months, on the slide; tried to push her off. Edith caught hold of Freda's curl and held it; Freda caught hold of Edith's plait and held it too, both children screaming.

So far as recognition of the consequences of aggressive acts is concerned, we can at that age distinguish three main phases. In the first, the child does not realize what harm his hostile acts may do to the other child. His own feelings — jealousy, envy — prompt him to take aggressive action, but his realization does not go beyond the relief which the outbreak provides for these feelings — examples 13 and 14. In the second phase, the child realizes that his enemy gets hurt or harmed, but he does not mind; he rather enjoys seeing the result he has produced, that is, seeing the other child cry — example 15. The third phase includes the feeling of being sorry for the other child and repentance for the action, either because of identification with the other's feelings — "he feels the hurt as I do" — or because of a common relationship to a mother figure — "he belongs to her and she would not like me to hurt him". The latter feelings are not strong enough to prevent the child from aggressive outbursts, but strong enough to lead to acts of reparation after the outburst has relieved his feelings — example 16.

13. Christopher, twelve months, hit and scratched his own twin brother, Charlie; Christopher's face remained peaceful, Charlie cried bitterly.

14. Larry, sixteen months, often took a toy away from another child. When that child cried, he was very surprised, and did not know what he had done.

15. Jessie, twenty months, hit Bessie, her twin sister; was proud of it.

16. Dick, two years three months, was in a phase of special aggressiveness towards other children. The expression on his face left no doubt about his enjoyment of every kind of hurt which he was able to inflict on others. This reaction changed slowly when he grew attached to a particular nurse. Once again he had attacked Ida, twenty-two months, and was found with a tuft of her hair between his fingers. The nurse reproached him for his conduct. He was repentant, went back to Ida, held his clenched fist over her head, opened out his fingers, and carefully returned the tuft of hair to the place where it belonged.

Reactions of this kind can be observed in family as well as residential life. But, as mentioned before, children who live in age groups have more frequent occasion to be jealous

— the more so when we try to give them mother substitutes — and they are in an almost continual state of envy which is occasioned by the necessity to share toys; therefore they appear to the casual observer to be more aggressive. It would be more accurate to say that they have more occasion to be aggressive. If to this we add the fact that their victims, of the same age, are at the same time more helpless and, for the same reasons, more aggressive than elder brothers and sisters would ever be, we shall be better able to understand why aggressive moods are so much in the foreground in a group of residential infants. It is of special interest to observe how hostilities seldom remain restricted to the two children between whom they started, and how quickly they spread and include others who in the beginning took no part in the outbreak of the quarrel — examples 17 and 18.

17. Paul, twenty-three months, snatched Sophie's, nineteen months, teddy bear whereupon Sophie cried. Edith, twenty-one months, rushed to Sophie to hit her, and Sophie pulled Edith's dress; Edith cried and pulled Sophie's hair. Agnes, eighteen months, joined in the fight and came and pulled Sophie's and Edith's hair, whereupon Edith pushed Agnes until she screamed. Next Larry, nineteen months, joined in the fight, he went over to Agnes and pushed her over. In the meantime Edith had recovered and hit Larry until he pulled her hair so that she screamed. While all this was going on, Sam, twenty-three months, came by, petted Edith's hair and made affectionate noises.

18. Sophie, seventeen months, played peacefully with a doll's cup. Sam, twenty-one months, took it away; Sophie screamed but began to play with another toy after

a short time. Edith, nineteen months, was after the same cup and tried to take it from Sam; they fought until Edith was victorious and ran away with the cup. Sam lay down on the floor screaming, then got up, took the empty posting-box and tried to hammer with it on Edith's head. Edith lay down on the floor, kicked and screamed, but held on to the cup. Ivy, nineteen months, joined in, sat on top of Edith, pulled her hair, tore the cup away from her and ran off with it. Edith recovered after a while and tried to recapture the cup from Ivy. While they fought on the floor, Agnes, sixteen months, crawled over to them and took the cup away. Edith tried to get it back, but Agnes stood firm. There stood Ivy, her arms hanging limp in resignation, crying, Edith cried, and Sam and Sophie cried because Sam had tripped over Sophie. Only Agnes stood, holding on to a cot with one hand to steady herself, and waved the cup victoriously with the other hand.

OTHER CHILDREN TREATED AS A MENACE.
METHODS OF DEFENCE ADOPTED AGAINST THEM.

It is a known fact, though perhaps not sufficiently stressed, that the ability to defend one self develops later than the ability to attack. The same infants who can be very aggressive when prompted by their jealous or envious feelings, who bite, hit and push in the manner described above, suddenly stand helpless, cry and run for protection when attacked by others. Often they seem amazed or surprised at the aggressive act of another child, though they themselves have committed similar acts only a few minutes earlier.

Sensible methods of defense, by act or word, develop slowly and are seldom fully established before the third year. Some of our bigger boys, four-five years old, though very aggressive, can still do no more than attack others, and burst into tears as soon as they themselves are attacked. On the other hand some of the following examples show that occasionally very small infants deal successfully with aggressors, and, by their own determination, force them to abandon hostile intentions — examples 19 to 24.

19. Ivy, eighteen months, had developed the habit of sitting on Edith's, eighteen months, head whenever she found her lying on the floor. Edith always cried, but never tried to defend herself nor to escape.

20. Sam, twenty-one months, was playing peacefully, when suddenly Larry, nineteen months, took his ball away. Sam looked at his empty hands helplessly and began to cry.

21. Paul, two years, was very clever in building. He built towers as high as himself out of very small bricks. While building, he was always afraid lest some other child might push his tower over. This disturbed his concentration; he kept looking nervously in all directions for approaching enemies. When any child dared to come near, Paul rushed at it, and pushed it over with one quick and energetic movement. When, in spite of all precautions, his tower fell over, Paul lay down on the floor in despair and cried for a long time. Then he sucked his two fingers and started to build again, still sobbing. This procedure was repeated innumerable times.

22. Sophie, nineteen months, slowly ascended the steps of the slide. Larry, twenty months, who followed her and wanted to be quicker than Sophie, pushed her. But

Sophie turned round, said "no, no," and pulled his hair.

23. Sam, twenty-two months, was building with two stools; he needed a third, but Agnes, nineteen months, was sitting on it. Sam walked over to Agnes and looked at her with pleading eyes for about half a minute. Agnes fixed her eyes on Sam but did not move. So Sam's eyes became sad, he sucked his thumb and retired slowly.

24. Sophie, nineteen months, had a rusk in her hand which Larry, nineteen months, wanted badly. She began to scream as soon as Larry approached her, evidently guessing his evil intentions. When she screamed, Larry withdrew his hand. He began to busy himself with a teddy bear which was lying between them, played with it and pointed at its eyes, but had his own eyes fixed on the rusk all the time. He tried repeatedly for an opportunity to snatch the rusk; but Sophie did not give him a chance. Finally, he walked away disappointed.

OTHER CHILDREN CONSOLED, COMFORTED, SOOTHED.

Though infants are quick to hurt each other they are equally quick to pity another child, and to make amends to him for what has happened, especially when the aggressive act has not been committed by them but by a third party. In these acts of "pity" they are evidently moved by an identification with the emotions shown by the victim. Examples 27 and 28 seem to prove that there is little difference between comforting another child and comforting oneself. Identification with the victim is further shown in many instances by the adoption of a hostile attitude towards the aggressor. Thus, the infant who consoles or comforts another often combines a friendly act towards the victim with an aggressive one towards the aggressor.

25. Violet, two years four months, sat in a corner crying. Agnes, nineteen months, suddenly rushed to the next toy-box, took out two toys, gave them quickly to Violet and ran away again. This was the first occasion of her being "helpful."

26. Sam, twenty-two months, had just stopped crying but looked unhappy still, when Rose, twenty-two months, entered the room. She was evidently struck by his expression, watched him critically for a moment, and then ran to him and petted him.

27. Rose, twenty-one months, watched Edith, twenty-two months, petting Sam, twenty-two months, who was crying. She went to Sam and petted him too, then went to Edith and Freda, twenty-two months, and petted them, and finally she stroked her own hair and cheek and, with a radiant smile, made affectionate noises to herself.

28. The junior toddlers were waiting for their tea in the afternoon. Charlie, twenty-three months, and Paul, two years, sat at the same table. Paul played with a little tin box which Charlie wanted to get from him. When he tried to reach it, he caught his finger in it and began to cry. Paul saw that Charlie was hurt, immediately lifted his own finger and put it into Charlie's mouth to comfort him.

29. Edith, twenty-one months, had been hurt by Paul, twenty-three months, and cried terribly. When Sam, twenty months, saw Edith unhappy, he came to comfort her. Larry, nineteen months, watched the scene and went to help Sam to comfort Edith.

30. Jeffrey, two years five months, fell off the push-dog and cried bitterly. Bridget, two years eight months, rushed to the dog, hit it and shook it until it fell over. Then she picked it up again, hit it once more and then seemed satisfied.

31. Sam, twenty-one months, was playing peacefully (see example 20), when suddenly Larry, nineteen months, took his ball away. Sam looked at his empty hands helplessly and began to cry. Edith, twenty-one months, had watched this scene; she rushed over to Larry, bit him, took the ball away from him, brought the ball back to Sam, and stroked his hair until he was comforted.

32. Dick, two and one-half years, who went through a phase of special aggressiveness, wanted to have a toy bus with which Irwin, two and one-quarter years, was playing. He threw himself on Irwin and knocked him down. Irwin fell unluckily and cut his lip on the toy. The nurse comforted him and showed Dick what he had done. Dick was obviously frightened and looked at Irwin with wide eyes. Then he looked round the room, saw Kitty, two and one-half years, holding a doll, ran to her, knocked her over, took the doll from her and gave it to Irwin, saying: "Poor Irwin, poor Irwin, have dolly." The nurse showed him that Kitty was crying now and tried to make him understand that it was nice of him to try to comfort Irwin with the doll, but that he could have found a toy to give him without hurting Kitty. But Dick did not seem to understand. He repeated several times: "Kitty naughty girl," because she did not want to surrender the doll; he was exclusively concerned with Irwin's bleeding lip.

INFANTS HELPING EACH OTHER.

The same attitude which leads to the acts of consolation just described, prompts the children to help each other in all the various tasks of everyday life. On the basis of the same needs and wishes, one infant perfectly understands and identifies himself with the difficulties and desires of the other children.

33. Jock, fourteen months, cried because he had lost his rusk and could not find it again. Sam, twenty-one months, walked over to him, found the rusk on the floor and gave it to him.

34. Rose, nineteen months, sat at a table and drank her cocoa. Edith, seventeen months, climbed up and tried to take the mug from Rose's mouth. Rose looked at her in surprise, then turned the mug and held it for Edith so that she could drink the cocoa.

35. Jessie, two years, was pushing a doll's pram around the garden. When she came to the corner of the path, she could not turn, pushed hard against the edge of the path and then began to cry. Bessie, her twin sister, came to the rescue and pushed the pram around the corner for her. A short while later Bessie was pushing the pram, got stuck at the same corner and cried. This time Jessie came and turned the pram around the corner for her. Each seemed able to do for the other what she could not accomplish for herself.

36. Edith, twenty-one months, had taken off her shoe and sock and tried hard to put them on again. Paul, twenty-three months, watched her from a distance, then rushed over to her, sat down on the floor and took the sock out of her hand. He tried with surprising patience

to put it on Edith's foot, his mouth open, his tongue far out, breathing heavily. Edith watched his face and immediately imitated his expression. For two or three minutes both children were absorbed in their occupation and had an expression of the utmost strain on their faces.

37. Nurse Jean fetched Bridget, two years, from the shelter dormitory in the morning. Since the dressing room upstairs was already full of children, she only took that one child. When passing other beds, Bridget heard Jeffrey, two years, cry. She stopped and said: "Jeffrey crying, Jean." The nurse explained that Jeffrey would have to wait a little, and proceeded to take Bridget upstairs. Suddenly on the middle of the staircase, Bridget turned round, said: "I go to Jeffrey," and went back. The nurse waited for her to return, but then followed her to see what had happened. In the meantime Bridget had opened the net of Jeffrey's bed, so that he could get out, and had pushed the step-ladder to Bill's, two years nine months, bed to let him get out; she was just about to push the steps to Dan's, two years eight months, bed. She was holding his hand and saying: "not fall down".

DIRECT EDUCATIONAL INFLUENCE OF INFANTS
ON EACH OTHER.

RESTRICTION OF AGGRESSION, GREED, DIRTY HABITS, ETC.
It is common knowledge that children educate each other and that, in families, the influence of elder brothers and sisters makes itself strongly felt as an addition to the educational influence of the parents. Many children who are unwilling to obey their parents are quite ready to obey the commands and prohibitions of older children. Imitation of

examples set by older children seems easier, and their re-
bukes or even punishments, though effective, seem to hurt
less. This educational help rendered by elder brothers and
sisters is one of the reasons why the whole process of upbringing is smoother where the family is large.

But this type of "education" through the agency of older
children is very different from the influence which infants
in the same age group exert on each other. Whereas older
brothers and sisters act as parent substitutes — parent
figures on a reduced scale — these contemporaries in an
age group are equals in status. One child can influence
the other if at that moment he is the stronger one, i.e.
because at that moment he is a menace to the other child;
the latter will then obey him out of fear. Or, one infant
can influence the other because at that moment he is further
advanced in some achievement — walking, habit training,
etc. The position will be reversed when another achievement plays the greater role in which the second child sur-
passes the first. That means that the children influence each
other on the basis of superior strength or superior achievement. Fear of each other and admiration for each other
are the deciding factors in this respect. Observation shows
that, owing to these interrelations between the infants, certain results are produced which at the first glance are not
very different from the results produced by education
proper: aggression is checked, wish fulfilment is postponed
and certain "good habits" are acquired under the pressure
of these circumstances.

38. Freda, twenty-one months, pulled Sam's hair.
Sam, twenty-one months, cried but did not defend himself. Jeffrey, 2 years four months, crossed the nursery
quickly, hit Freda twice, and then comforted Sam. When

Sam stopped crying, Jeffrey once more turned to Freda and looked at her with indignation, whereupon Freda immediately shrank back into a corner. Then Jeffrey walked away, obviously pleased with himself.

In this case it is clear why Jeffrey can exert such influence. He is seven months older and considerably stronger than Freda. Since he would not hesitate a moment to use his superior strength, he constitutes a very real danger to Freda. She checks her aggression out of fear.

39. Sam, twenty-one months, built with bricks in a corner of the room. Freda, twenty-one months, approached him carefully, with the obvious intention of destroying his building. Sam looked up and said: "No, no." Freda changed her intention: she hesitated for a moment, then picked up a brick and gave it to Sam; slowly she collected all the bricks in the room and handed them to Sam in succession.

In this case the result achieved is due to other causes. Sam and Freda are at the same age; there is no difference in strength between them; Sam is a particularly gentle child who is not feared by anybody. This time Freda does not stop her destructive action out of fear. She is impressed by Sam's unexpected determination to a degree which changes her destructive intention to its opposite. She now helps him instead of harming him.

40. Bessie, nineteen months, had a comb in her hand, Jessie, her twin sister, a toy with which she played. Bessie wanted the toy but checked her impulse to take it. Suddenly she offered the comb to Jessie; Jessie took it quietly and surrendered the desired toy. There was not a sound from either of them while this exchange took place.

All children in our groups learn very early that to snatch

a toy from another child invites trouble, i.e. an outbreak
of resentment or unhappiness from the victim. The method
adopted most frequently is exchange: they offer something
with one hand and take away with the other. Again, as in
former instances, this gesture is only apparently altruistic;
it signifies restraint of greed or aggression acquired under
the pressure of bitter experience. Occurrences of this kind
may be observed in our nursery constantly. For instance:

41. Maggie, two years, cried because Dinah, her sister,
three years, had snatched a toy from her. Bridget, two
years, who had witnessed the scene, tried to restore order.
She snatched away the toy from Dinah and returned it
to Maggie. When Dinah now threw herself on the floor
and cried, Bridget went to look for a substiute, found
an old toilet paper roll and brought it to Dinah. When
Dinah refused it, she gave it to Maggie, taking the toy
at the same time from Maggie to bring it to Dinah. To
Bridget's great concern Maggie now cried as well as
Dinah. That was too much for her. First she hit both,
then tried to comfort both and when nothing helped she
gave up.

42. Carol, three and one-half years, tried to snatch a
doll from Jessie, two years. Jessie bit her so that she
had to let the doll go. Bessie, Jessie's twin sister, came
to the rescue and hit Carol from behind. Jessie suddenly
stopped biting and shouted: "No, no, Bessie, not hit."
It is not clear in this case why in Jessie's code which she
tries to impart to Bessie, biting is allowed but hitting forbidden.

43. Bridget, two years four months, and Dick, three
years, were sitting together at breakfast. They talked to
each other happily until Dick began to smear his porridge

all over the table. Bridget wrinkled her nose in disgust: "Stop it, Dicky, you dirty boy." Dick: "No, I won't." Bridget, very cross: "Dicky, I don't like it, you naughty." Dick, shouting: "No." Bridget, very angry indeed, disgust in her face: "Dicky, I won't sit with you any more. I sit with Marion (the nurse)." She picked up her plate and mug and dragged her chair over to the nurse, muttering and grumbling all the time at Dick.

In this instance, Bridget, though younger, assumes educational superiority on the basis of her better manners. She has just completed her habit training, but has become at the same time very intolerant towards all children who are not quite up to her standards of cleanliness in either lavatory or table manners.

The position between the two children is reversed in the following instance, two months later.

44. Bridget joined the dinner of the bigger children for the first time and did not know how to handle a fork. Her friend Dick watched her at first and then said: "Not like that, Bridget, look at me." Bridget looked at him and copied him carefully right through the meal.

The following two examples demonstrate how consideration of the other child, based on identification with his desires, leads to real acts of sacrifice and generosity. Aggression in these cases is completely checked.

45. Sam, twenty-one months, held a piece of paper in front of his face and played "peek-a-bo." Sophie, twenty months, wanted the paper and screamed. So Sam tore the paper in two and gave one part to her. Then both children played "peek-a-bo"; they did it in turns and laughed heartily.

46. Jeffrey, two years four months, returned from a walk with a new book which he had been given as a present. He was delighted with it and showed it to everybody. When Teddy, two years one month, saw the nice book, he took it away. Jeffrey screamed, ran after him, and recovered it. Teddy immediately began to cry disconsolately until Jeffrey gave him the book again. Teddy stopped crying but Jeffrey now did not dare take his property away again. So they both sat down and looked at it together. Teddy kept the book all afternoon.

Friendship Between Infants.

Under ordinary conditions friendships of long duration are believed to be very rare among young children. Lasting attachments are formed to grown-ups or to older children; playmates of the same age are used for purposes of play only, and friendships fall apart when the momentary reason for them — the play — has ended.

Matters are different under residential conditions. We observe many instances of friendship among infants which last days, weeks, or even months. Playmates are certainly not chosen indiscriminately; in playing together the partner often seems no less important than the game. Partnership of this kind is most outstanding in several pairs of twins who live in our nursery. It is interesting to note that this natural partnership, which appears in twins, develops in a similar manner, only quantitively less, in many residential infants.

47. Reggie, eighteen to twenty months, and Jeffrey, fifteen to seventeen months, had become great friends. They always played with each other and hardly ever took

notice of another child. This friendship had lasted about two months when Reggie went home. Jeffrey missed him very much; he hardly played during the following days and sucked his thumb more than usual.

48. Sophie, nineteen months, and Larry, nineteen months, had founded a building society. Whenever one of them started building, the other joined in quickly, and then they built in turns, each putting a brick carefully on the tower and then waiting until the other had put his brick on. They used 10 to 12 bricks and were very happy in their companionship.

49. Sophie, nineteen months, loved to sit in a certain cupboard. When she wanted company, and when the right child was near her, she called energetically "More, more," and pointed at the empty space next to her. She usually invited Edith, twenty-one months, or Agnes, eighteen months. As soon as the invited child sat down beside her, Sophie began to bang her feet on the floor and the other child joined in. If an unwanted child tried to sit in the cupboard, Sophie quickly pushed it away with a loud "No, no."

50. Bessie, twenty-two months, became very submissive to Tom, two years. For weeks she helped him in all his occupations and joined in all his games. She carried bricks for him when he was building and placed the chairs for him when he was playing train. He was grateful for her services, and returned them occassionally. For instance, when Bessie once tried to climb on a chair and got into a rather awkward position, he suddenly appeared and held the chair for her.

51. Several junior toddlers were playing on the floor. Sophie, fifteen months, got upset by another child and

began to cry bitterly; nothing could comfort her, she just cried and cried. Terry, twenty months, came up to her and looked into her face. She took no notice and went on crying. Terry was very puzzled and began to shake his head; he shook it so violently that he sat down on the floor with a big bump. He laughed and Sophie stopped crying for a second, then started again. Terry got up, shook his head and bumped down again with a loud laugh. Sophie smiled and forgot to cry. Terry repeated this performance as many as fourteen times. He was nearly worn out and quite dizzy, both children shaking with laughter. The other children got interested, but as soon as they came near, he stopped and even pushed one of them away, to start again when he and Sophie were left alone.

INSTANCES OF LOVE-PLAY, TENDERNESS, AFFECTION.

The following examples show behavior between infants which is hardly different from the expressions of love and affection between adults.

52. The nurse who entered the rest room during the children's afternoon nap found Paul, two years, and Sophie, nineteen months, standing at one end of their cots kissing each other. She was amused and laughed. Paul turned around and smiled at her for a moment, then again held Sophie's head between both his hands and kissed her over and over again. Sophie smiled and was obviously pleased.

53. This love scene between Paul and Sophie had its continuation. Sophie's favorite toy was a brown teddy. Paul had learned that he could make her unhappy by

taking the teddy away and stop her unhappiness by returning it to her. Five days after the kissing incident
he used this knowledge to attract her attention specially.
He took the teddy away and Sophie began to cry. He
ran to the other end of the nursery and then back to
Sophie, returned the teddy to her and was very pleased.
He repeated this at least ten times during the afternoon.

54. Ivy, twenty months, and Agnes, fifteen months,
were taken out in the pram. They played with each other
and kissed and hugged each other most of the time. Ivy
was the one who started it over and over again and
Agnes responded. Both children laughed with pleasure.

55. Sophie, twenty months, stood in a corner of the
nursery and looked at Larry, nineteen months. Larry
noticed her and went to her saying "Ay! ay!" Sophie
put her arms around Larry. They stayed like that for
quite a while.

56. Tom, twenty months, and Stella, seventeen months,
played with each other on the floor. Suddenly Tom
pushed Stella over so that she lay on her back, her hands
under her head. He climbed on her and rocked. Both
children looked perfectly happy. Then Tom got up and
walked away and Stella looked at him once more and
got up too. When, in the afternoon, Tom entered the
nursery Stella immediately lay down on the floor again
and resumed the position of the morning. She looked
at Tom in an expectant manner but got up when he took
no notice.

57. Henry, two years seven months, and Ralph, three
years four months, have had a friendship of long standing. One morning Ralph was looking at a "story book",
pointed excitedly to the capital B on the title page and

called out: "Look, look, that's Henry and me". The whole morning he looked at books in the nursery and every time when he saw a capital B he said over and over again: "That's Henry and me".

The form of the letter B suggested to him the picture of two friends embracing each other.

INTRODUCTION OF THE MOTHER-RELATION-SHIP INTO NURSERY-LIFE

IT is a fallacy to conclude that the variety of emotions which the young child in a residential nursery develops towards the playmates of its own age-group, can make up in any way for the emotions which it would normally direct towards its parents. The latter remain undeveloped and unsatisfied, but many observations show that they are latent in the child and ready to leap into action the moment the slightest opportunity for attachment is offered by the outward circumstances. This is all the more noticeable, the less a child has knowledge of, or opportunity to form an emotional attachment to, its own mother.

FORMATION OF ARTIFICIAL FAMILIES.

We have repeatedly made the experiment of dividing up some large "age groups" of children into small units of 3, 4 or 5 under the guidance of one young nurse or teacher who acted as their foster mother where motherly care was concerned. In all these instances the group reactions of the children quickly changed to the emotional reactions of children in a natural family setting. They formed a strong and possessive attachment to their nurse and were at the same time more exacting, but also more willing to make sacrifices for her, than they had been before. Certain steps in development which had been difficult or impossible in the group setting, as for instance habit training, were under these changed conditions easier to accomplish. The other children of the same "family" were then treated with the mixture of jealousy and toleration which is one of the characteristics of the brother-sister relationship; but this tolerance was not extended outside the family. The children quickly developed an understanding of the other families and respected each other's rights to the possession of a particular grown-up. The younger children express all these reactions in their behavior, the older children very clearly with the help of speech. They talk about their "own" nurses as if they were precious possessions, compare them with each other or boast of them as other children do of their mothers, etc. Artificial families are usually arranged so that two nurses substitute for each other on their off-days, and children treat this substitute foster mother with a lesser degree of possessiveness, but still as something of their own.

1. Derrick, three years nine months, said on his way home from a walk: "When my Sara is off, it's my Martha, and when my Martha is off, it is my Sara." Arrived in the house, he did not find Sara, so he said at once: "My Sara is all gone, my Martha now." Derrick is an extremely difficult problem child who hardly lets himself be touched by anybody except "his Sara", or in the second place "his Martha".

2. Bridget, two and one-half years, belonged to the family of Nurse Jean of whom she was extremely fond. When Jean had been ill for a few days and returned to the nursery, she constantly repeated: "My Jean, my Jean". Lillian, two and one-half years, once said "my Jean" too, but Bridget objected and explained: "It's my Jean, it's Lillian's Ruth and Keith's very own Ilsa".

3. Conversation between Bridget, two years eight months, and Jeffrey, two years six months. When Bridget returned from the measles sickroom, where she had been separated from Jean, she was more jealous than ever and did not allow Jeffrey even to mention Nurse Jean's name without saying "It's my Jean". The first morning Jeffrey took it quietly, just looked at her and did not answer. In the afternoon he got upset about it, looked at Nurse Jean and began to cry. Jean explained to Bridget that it was quite true, that she was her Jean and that Jeffrey had his Sara, but that Sara was ill at the moment, so Jean had to look after Jeffrey until Sara was well again. Bridget seemed to understand, she played and did not mention the subject again until tea time, when she suddenly turned to Jeffrey and said: "It's my Jean, it's your Sara, Jeffrey, isn't it? All right?" Whereupon Jeffrey said: "All right, my Sara". Next day at lunch when the children were sitting next to each other again, Bridget restarted the subject in a very provocative way: "It's my Jean". Jeffrey hit her with his spoon and said in a furious voice: "Your Jean". Bridget was so pleased with her success that she did not even complain about being hit.

Acceptance of the family grouping also produces a certain amount of reserve and resentment on the part of the children, which makes itself felt specially when the mother of one family tries to help or take care of members of another. But reactions of this kind are confined to such intimate ministrations as for instance undressing, potting and bathing.

4. When Nurse Ilsa asked Christine, four years, one night whether she would like to be bathed by her, Chris-

tine said: "No, 'cause you don't know how to bath girls. you can only bath Bob and Martin."

5. When Nurse Ursula wanted to bath Kitty one evening, Kitty refused and said: "You like to bath Jessie and Bessie." She repeated this several times and was persistent in her refusal.

As mentioned before, these family arrangements are restricted to the motherly care of the children and do not extend to their occupations during the day. But some children even insist on being reproached or corrected only by their "own" people.

6. Bridget, two years eight months, when told by another nurse that she had done something wrong and that this was "not nice at all", only gave her a furious look, stamped her foot and shouted: "My Jean." (It was Jean's day off.)

7. Tony, four years, was told by a nurse to get off the window-sill on which he was standing. He got most indignant about it. He said: "Don't talk to me like that. Sister Mary does not! You have to say, please come down from the window-sill."

Some children show and express great understanding of the others in this respect.

8. When Derrick, three years, was cross with Nurse Ilsa and threatened "I'll put you in the water" (the most popular threat used by the children), Shirley, four years nine months, said: "No, Derrick, you can't do that, 'cause Bob" (who is in Ilsa's family) "won't have no Ilsa left and he needs one."

9. Shirley, four years ten months, said at night in bed: "I have a very nice mummy. I like her very much. Mrs. B. is a nice mummy and Mrs. G. too. All children

have nice mummies, but Hannah" (a young nurse) "must come to see her Kitty on Sundays and bring her cake. Kitty has no nice mummy, that's why she has her Hannah."

Specific Nature and Consequences of the Mother-Relationship.

Repeated experience proves the importance of the introduction of this substitute mother-relationship into the life of a residential nursery. A child who forms this kind of relationship to a grown-up not only becomes amenable to educational influence in a very welcome manner, but shows more vivid and varied facial expressions, develops individual qualities and unfolds his whole personality in a surprising way. On the other hand it has to be admitted that family arrangements of this kind introduce very many disturbing and complicating elements into nursery life. Children, who have shown themselves adaptable and accommodating under group conditions, suddenly become insufferably demanding and unreasonable. Their jealousy and, above all, their possessiveness of the beloved grown-up may be boundless. It easily becomes compulsive where the mother-relationship is no new experience but where separation from a real mother or (and) a former foster-mother has occurred before. The child is all the more clinging, the more it has an inner conviction that separation will repeat itself. Children become disturbed in their play activities when they watch anxiously whether their "own" nurse leaves the room on an errand or for her off-hour or whether she has any intimate dealings with children outside her family. Tony, three and one-half, for instance, would not allow Sister

Mary to use "his" hand for handling other children. Jim, two to three, would burst into tears whenever his "own" nurse left the room. Shirley, four years, would become intensely depressed and disturbed when "her" Marion was absent for some reason, etc. It is true that all these children had had to cope with a series of traumatic separations in their lives.

It is of the greatest interest to watch the difference of behavior shown by the children in these intimate relations with their chosen foster-mothers on the one hand and with the group teacher in the nursery on the other. We are in this respect often reminded of the difference of behavior which children, who live with their families, show in the day-nursery. They are sometimes perfectly good and social in the nursery and extremely difficult at home. This is not — as many nursery-school teachers seem to think — due to the fact that the mother does not know how to handle the child whereas the teacher does. It is due to the difference in the emotional response to mother and teacher respectively, a difference which we find reflected in the different response to the "family mother" and the group teacher in a residential home. The mother-relationship or its substitute awakens emotions in the child which in their turn give rise to passionate demands which clamor for satisfaction. This first and early love reaction to a mother enriches the life of the child by laying the foundations for all future love-relationships. Like all love, it entails a wealth of complications, conflicts, disappointments and frustrations. The child is usually quite unable to express or even consciously to realize the nature and extent of his demand on the mother or mother substitute. It displaces this unconscious wish to all sorts of substitute gratifications, none of which — even if capable of fulfilment — will ever satisfy his need.

10. Jim was separated from a very nice and affectionate mother at seventeen months and developed well in our nursery. During his stay he formed two strong attachments to two young nurses who successively took care of him. Though he was otherwise a well adjusted, active and companionable child, his behavior became impossible where these attachments were concerned. He was clinging, over-possessive, unwilling to be left for a minute, and continually demanded something without being able to define in any way what it was he wanted. It was no unusual sight to see Jim lie on the floor sobbing and despairing. These reactions ceased when his favorite nurse was absent even for short periods. He was then quiet and impersonal. Love on the one hand, and an intense feeling of frustration on the other, seemed inextricably bound up with each other in his case.

11. Martin, who came to our nursery at sixteen months, formed a similar kind of attachment to his beloved Ilsa from the moment when he entered her group at approximately two years. He was an especially healthy and robust child, full of fun, active and mischievous. In his relations with Ilsa he would turn into a passive and clinging baby at the slightest provocation. This behavior became intensified when he was about three years. Whenever he came home to Netherhall Gardens from the nursery class which we run for our children in Wedderburn Road, he apparently thought that he could spend the rest of the day constantly in Ilsa's company. Whenever this was not possible, he flew into violent tempers and lay on the floor crying for long times. On a certain day he was more of a tyrant than ever before,

obviously looking for trouble. When Ilsa told him to put on shoes, he wanted boots; when he got cake, he wanted chocolate; when Ilsa wanted to bath him in the big tub which he usually loves, he asked for the little one. He was exhausted when he was in bed at last, sent her away without "good night" and then cried because she had not said "good night". After such scenes he stammered badly for several hours, sometimes for a whole day.

The next morning he started off in a similar manner. When at breakfast he said he did not like "that sugar" on the cornflakes and when Ilsa asked what kind of sugar he wanted, he stamped his foot and stuttered: "Bl—black sugar". When he saw her laugh, he suddenly roared with laughter himself, said very sensibly, "There is no black sugar", and was perfectly all right for the rest of the day.

12. Readers who are familiar with our monthly reports will remember similar reactions which Tony, then three and one-half years, developed in the beginning of his intimacy with Sister Mary. He would send her out of the room in the evening when she offered to stay with him and call her back in despair as soon as she had left him. He would accuse her that she had hurt him in some way or neglected his small hurts or ailments. He would wake up in the middle of the night and complain to the night nurse that Sister Mary had not said "good night" to him, in spite of the fact that she had done so, had looked after him and fulfilled his wishes to the best of her ability. At four and one half, when he was going through a difficult time owing to the remarriage of his father, he would suddenly interrupt his play, search for

her and say over and over again: "I want to tell you something. I want to tell you something." When asked what he wanted to tell, he did not know. Sometimes he said: "I want to kiss you", but it was quite clear that the kiss was not his real reason and that the real nature of his demand was not known to him.

Behavior of this kind is naturally not welcome in the nursery. It acts as a disturbance to the other children and is often criticized sharply by the other members of the staff who cannot help but feel that this particular nurse has "spoilt" this child and that the child would be much better off, i.e. much quieter without the disturbing complications of this intimate relationship. This is only true in the sense in which we would all be better off, i.e. more sensible, without emotions. In reality it is not the absence of irrational emotional attachments which helps a child to grow up normally but the painful and often disturbing process of learning how to deal with such emotions.

As stated earlier, even the secure and uninterrupted relationship of a small child to his parents is full of conflicts, disappointments and unfulfilled longings. The child wants to possess father or mother exclusively and in every sense of the word, which it cannot do. Restrictions of the child's demands are taken as rebuff, the necessary refusal of bodily intimacy creates unhappiness, guilt and inhibition. Comparison with the parent of the same sex brings home to the child a sense of his own smallness and inefficiency.

The first family setting is the framework within which the instincts and emotions of the child grope towards their first objects. The child can never completely possess these objects but in this first display of its feelings it learns "to love", to cope with its instinctual forces and thus lay the foundations for its character formation, a process which entails a great deal of discomfort. It is this first parent-relationship which the child repeats, sometimes in a lessened, sometimes in in an intensified degree on the parent-substitutes, if they are offered to it, in a residential institution.

FURTHER CONSEQUENCES OF THE SUBSTITUTE MOTHER-RELATIONSHIP IN THE NURSERY.

The introduction of the mother-relationship into nursery life, necessary as it seems to us, is not only accompanied by all the disturbing emotional elements described above, but further brings with it the danger of renewed separation.

Nurses do leave at times or, in the course of their training, change from department to department, and separations of this kind, when an intimate attachment has been formed, are frequently not less painful than the initial separation from the mother. Here the child again displays all the conflicting emotions of sorrow, longing and resentment which we have described as involved in the separation from the mother. Examples of this kind are countless. Especially recent and striking is the following.

13. Reggie, who had come to our house as a baby of five months, went home to his mother when he was one year eight months, and has been with us ever since his return to the nursery two months later. While with us, he formed two passionate relationships to two young nurses who took care of him at different periods. The second attachment was suddenly broken at two years eight months when his "own" nurse married. He was completely lost and desperate after her departure, and refused to look at her when she visited him a fortnight

later. He turned his head to the other side when she spoke to him, but stared at the door, which had closed behind her, after she had left the room. In the evening in bed he sat up and said: "My very own Mary-Ann! But I don't like her."

The fact that such renewed separations are bound to happen is often used as an argument against family arrangements in the nursery. But argumentation of this kind seems to us erroneous. When choosing between the two evils of broken and interrupted attachments and an existence of emotional barrenness, the latter is the more harmful solution because, as will be shown later, it offers less prospect for normal character development.

SPONTANEOUS ATTACHMENT TO A GROWN UP.

We have shown before how quickly the latent parent-child relationship becomes manifest, for instance, when opportunity is offered through formation of artificial family groups. These inner urges of the child do not always wait for carefully thought out arrangements. They arise in answer to actions of the grown-ups: whoever merely takes care of a child for any length of time in a motherly way, may easily become the chosen foster-mother of this child. But children choose their foster-mothers too where no previous action on the part of the grown-up has provoked the process; it seems at first sight as if they choose at random. Closer investigation of every such occurrence shows that these apparently spontaneous attachments of the children really arise in answer to a feeling in the adult person, in many cases a feeling of which the adult was not aware in the beginning, or the reasons for which only became apparent after some searching.

A young nurse for instance felt attracted to one of the liveliest little boys in the nursery. When questioning herself she found that he resembled the favorite brother of her childhood. Another nurse felt attracted to a child whose tragic loss of his parents reminded her of her own tragic separation from her family. Another one felt specially drawn to small girls whose family constellation reminded her of her own position in her family with all its consequences, etc. In all these instances the children answered this hardly conscious attitude with violent attachments from their own side. It seemed as if the emotion that lay dormant in them had only waited for an answering spark in some adult person to flare up.

It is essential for all people who live and work in close contact with children to realize the existence of these emotional moves in themselves and through realization gain control over them. Though the adult in the nursery serves as object and outlet for the emotions which lie ready in the child, the children should on no account serve as outlets for the uncontrolled and therefore unrestrained emotions of the adults, irrespective of whether these emotions are of a positive or negative kind.

SOME ASPECTS OF INSTINCTUAL SATISFAC-
TION AND FRUSTRATION IN FAMILY-
AND NURSERY-LIFE

IN our former chapters we tried to establish one main fact: that small infants in a residential nursery, though they develop community reactions and enjoy the companionship of children of their own age, search further for objects towards whom they can direct all those emotional interests which they would normally direct towards their parents. We have described how the grown-ups of the nursery are turned into parent-substitutes. It is our next task to discuss how far these emotional relationships satisfy the natural desires of the child and how far they are destined to fail in this respect.

Bodily Intimacy Between Infant and Mother.

It is a well known fact that small infants treat parts of the mother's body as if they were their own. The baby, for instance, first experiences the pleasurable sensation of sucking while feeding at the mother's breast. When it wants the same pleasure between feeds, i.e. at times when the mother's breast is not at its disposal, it substitutes its own finger, or fingers, for the nipple. We assume that in the beginning it does not discriminate between what belongs to its own body and what to the mother's and that probably the discovery that its own hand is always present whereas the mother's breast periodically disappears, serves as the first distinction between a body of one's own and an outer world.

The infant plays with the mother in the same ways in which it plays with itself. It pulls her hair, pokes its finger into her eyes, her nose, mouth and ears or plays with her fingers; similarly it plays on its own face and with its own hands. Pleasure is evidently gained both from its own body and from the mother's. Sometimes, in such a search for pleasure, the two are used in turn.

Some examples of this unity of body between child and motherly person are observed under nursery conditions as well.

1. Lily, from the age of ten weeks, used to play for for a long time with her own hands. This became less frequent after the age of four months, when it gave way to play with her rattle or with the frill of her dress. But interest in hands was revived at eight months, when Lily began to play with the nurse's hand. The latter once rested quietly in the baby's cot and Lily suddenly touched it, held it and moved it a little, in turn. She laughed and kicked while doing so and became so excited that after a while the nurse had to remove her hand. She had never before reacted to any other incident in her life with as much happiness and excitement.

2. Rose had always, since babyhood, sucked her thumb before falling asleep. At twenty-one months she began the following bedtime plays with her favorite nurse. For several days she put her hand in the nurse's mouth and then fall asleep. In a next phase she would try to take the nurse's hand in her mouth. She would open it wide to get in as much of the big hand as possible. Another evening she was sucking her thumb in the usual way. Suddenly she nodded her head, took a corner of her blanket — the same corner which she always used to grasp

tightly during thumb-sucking —, tried to push it into the nurse's mouth, smiled contentedly and fell asleep.

3. Dick developed between the age of two and three, an unusual way of finding bodily satisfaction at bedtime, or when he wanted comfort after a temper. He grasped the forefinger of a person of whom he was fond, held it tightly, and tried to push it hard into the inside corner of his eye. His whole body became tense while doing so, and his face showed an expression of extreme pleasure. The fingers he tried to get hold of were those of four nurses with whom he was on specially good terms. He would occasionally use his own finger, but always tried to get hold of one of these others, if possible.

4. Jeffrey, between two and two years three months, developed various ways of playing with his favorite nurse. When she dressed him, he would explore her face; he would touch her eyes, in particular, and be delighted. When she bent her head to lace his shoes, he would put the forefinger of each of his hands into her ears and laugh with delight. Though, at this time, he had outgrown his violent thumb-sucking, he would resort to it, when being dressed before breakfast. Very frequently then he would lift his thumb and put it into the nurse's mouth. When she gave signs of not liking it, he would take her own thumb and put it into her own mouth. He had at this time just learned the first verse of Ba Ba Black Sheep. He loved to sing it, but instead of clapping his hands as the other children did, he would slap her face in the rhythm of the song. Whenever the doctor used a spatula to look at his throat, he would open his mouth willingly, but would try to make her take the other end of the spatula into her mouth.

This substitution of the mother's body for the small child's is even more frequent where the pleasure of eating is concerned. Mothers often describe proudly how "generous" their small children are, i.e. how willing to give them a bite of something which they are eating or to put a spoonful of food into their mouths when they are fed. They are usually surprised to see this early generosity disappear about the end of the second year and give way to a period of intense selfishness when the child wants to keep all the good things strictly to itself. It seems to us that, looked at more closely, this early generosity does not deserve its name; it has very little in common with the altruistic and self-denying quality which may appear in the same child two or three years later, as a result of character-development. The infant in its first two years does not really renounce pleasure to give to its mother; it is more correct to say that it fails to distinguish between itself and its mother. Pleasure given to the mother feels like pleasure given to itself, which means that the apparently altruistic action is, in reality, still egoistic. When the next step in development is made, and the mother definitely becomes part of the outside world, this first semblance of "generosity" naturally disappears.

Innumerable examples like the following may be observed. even under institutional conditions.

5. Violet, fourteen and one half months, was eating a biscuit. Several times she put it in the mouth of her favorite nurse as if it were her own.

6. Jeffrey, from early babyhood, found eating especially pleasureable. About the age of two to two and one half years, when he developed a special attachment to his new "family-mother," he expressed his oneness with her

not only by wanting to let her suck his finger, but as well by sharing his feeding pleasures with her. One day, for instance, he was eating a slice of apple. He held one end in his mouth and tried to push the other end into her mouth. Suddenly he pushed the whole slice into her mouth, looked at her laughingly, said "All gone," and was obviously pleased — an unheard of occurrence with Jeffrey who could never bear to be parted from his food. But in spite of his obvious greed, he would from then onwards, always try to feed this nurse with his lunch when she sat at his table. He may seem rather old for this reaction, but this delay is probably due to the fact that he has never lived with his mother and that this attachment to the new "family-mother" is the first close and steady relationship in his life.

It is not the purpose of these examples to show what close relationship to mother-substitutes the children may form in a nursery, or what possibilities for finding satisfaction are offered to them under those circumstances. Quite on the contrary, we take these individual occurrences as proof of the enormous strength of certain natural tendencies in the child, tendencies which under ordinary institutional conditions remain under the surface, and only betray themselves to the observer when certain conditions are fulfilled — as for instance formation of artificial families, isolation with one nurse in times of illness. Whatever efforts a residential nursery may make to offer "home care" to the infant, the lack in satisfaction given to these primitive desires will remain enormous. We are apt to forget it with those children who are completely under our care, i.e. homeless and motherless. It becomes obvious with all those who are visited by their mothers, and go home periodically to visit their families. Every one of our mothers, except those who are completely indifferent and neglectful, will fondle the child, usually far beyond the infant's momentary desire; she will handle it, far beyond the necessities of bodily care. Most of our children share a bed with their mother — some with the whole family — on their visits home and have done so before they came to us. When they return to the nursery, for instance after a Christmas holiday of two or three days and nights, sleeping alone is felt as a great hardship and deprivation. Some mothers certainly treat the child's body with possessiveness. They cannot leave it alone, kiss the child one minute, slap it the next, and continually interfere with its movements or its handling of its own body. The child is not supposed to put its finger into its mouth, or nose, or ears, to rub its eyes, to scratch itself, to masturbate, etc. But all the bodily stimulation which the mother interferes with on the one hand, is given to the child on the other hand through this incessant handling by the mother herself. We may assume on the basis of much evidence, that the child's feeling of oneness with the mother's body has a parallel in the mother's feeling that the child's body belongs to her.

To make our point quite clear: We are at the present moment not discussing whether this mother-child relationship is helpful or harmful to the infant, or what consequences these early experiences will have for later life. We merely show that these tendencies exist, that they find very full expression and satisfaction under home conditions, and that they are necessarily stunted and left largely unsatisfied in an institution. Nurses, however devoted and affectionate they may be, are taught to keep within the limits of objectivity. If they want to be successful as educationists, they have to work, not on the basis of their instinctive motherly feelings, but rather to develop and exchange these for a more general interest in the whole process of development of the children under their care.

AUTO-EROTIC HABITS IN A RESIDENTIAL INSTITUTION.

In our Annual Report*, we traced back the preponderance of auto-erotic habits in the nursery to the effect of sudden separation from the mother. What is true for children after the shock of separation, is certainly true for those who have been reared in an institution from babyhood. The infant's early desires, as described above, find their satisfaction partly on the mother, partly on its own body. When, as happens invariably in an institution, gratification derived from the substitute-mother relationship falls far short of what the child would normally experience, auto-erotic gratifications loom larger and fill the empty places in the child's instinctual life. With the small infants thumb-sucking, rocking and head-knocking take first place; masturbation, apart from its earliest appearance in babyhood, assumes importance at a slightly later stage.

Thumb-sucking. — We do not venture to say that sucking is really more prevalent in residential babies than in those who are brought up in families. Sucking for pleasure may be observed profusely under all conditions, though perhaps it is more striking to the observer where many babies are seen doing it in the same room and at the same time. A survey of sucking made at any one time in our baby-rooms shows that no two babies suck alike and that there is any amount of variety according to (*a*) the date

---

*War and Children, International University Press, 1944, New York,

when sucking begins; (*b*) the finger or fingers used; (*c*) the stereotyped position or playful activity of the other fingers during sucking; (*d*) the position or activity of the whole body during sucking; (*e*) the frequency and intensity of sucking with the individual baby; (*f*) damage done to the skin of the sucked parts, etc.

But, if there is little difference between private and residential babies during the sucking period itself, there is a conspicuous difference in the date of its termination. Residential infants tend to prolong sucking as a method of comforting themselves through several years of childhood, whereas children under home conditions outgrow this auto-erotic habit before the end of the second year.

Rocking. — Some of our infants begin to rock automatically whenever they are left alone in a confined space (crib, pram, play-pen), or when isolated for reasons of infectious disease. Toys are thrown out or disregarded at such times and the rhythmic movement of the body remains the sole occupation.

1. Freda, as a baby, lacked the usual interest in toys. From the age of six to ten months her only pleasure was a rhythmic movement of her whole body. At nine months, these movements were accompanied by all sorts of noises. At ten months the movements of the body ceased and only the rhythmic movements of the mouth remained. There was no gradual development of sitting, crawling and standing while the rhythmic movements were in action. But, at eleven months, after they had disappeared altogether, she learned to sit up, to kneel, to stand up and to walk round her cot all within a week.

2. Ivy, at ten months, rocked so continually in her cot in the baby-room, that she was transferred to the

junior-toddlers' department long before the usual time, in the hope that greater freedom of movement and more varied occupation would lessen the need for auto-erotic gratification. This worked at the time, but a year later automatic rocking combined with masturbation broke out in full force again at a time of prolonged illness with consequent restriction of movement.

3. Tom, between six and eight months, rocked so continually in the baby-room, that he was transferred to the next age group when only nine months old. His rocking ceased immediately and he became extremely skilful and energetic in movement and muscular control. Rocking returned temporarily a year later in a time of illness with consequent restriction of movement.

About the age of two years, he lost contact with his mother who abruptly ceased her visits to him. He became extremely dissatisfied and developed three rather disturbing reactions: violent thumb-sucking; over-eating; and passionate temporary attachments to strangers and guest-workers.

Head-knocking. — Head-knocking, according to our observations, appears about the age of one year, as a sign of frustration and impotent anger. At one period, when we had a specially persistent head-knocker in the junior-toddlers' room, it spread through imitation in a group of ten infants. Head-knocking is usually accompanied by crying. In some instances one might be led to believe, that the child cries as a result of the pain inflicted on it by knocking or banging its head. But closer observation shows that it is rather the other way round. The child first cries as an outlet for its anger or frustration and then follows up this expression with the more violent one of head-knocking.

4. Whenever Sidney, thirteen months, was thwarted in any way, he threw himself on his stomach, knocked his head violently and repeatedly on the floor and cried.

5. Christopher, at fourteen months, knocked his head against the top bar of his cot whenever he was cross. At fifteen months, during a period of illness and recovery, he did it constantly in a ferocious way, so that the nurse who took care of him, was in constant worry lest he might do himself more serious damage.

6. Charlie, thirteen months, knocked his head accidentally against the leg of a table while crawling round the room. He stopped in surprise, looked at the table leg, and tried to knock his head again, at first very gently, and then harder and harder with great concentration.

At sixteen months: He re-started head-knocking on the second day of an illness (pneumonia), but stopped the habit again after a week.

7. Babette, twelve to sixteen months.

At twelve months: On the first days, when she was put on the floor for crawling, she would often let her head drop forward and bang on the floor. This was at that time regarded as a sign of tiredness.

Several days later, she banged her head repeatedly until she got red marks. She was stopped, but it was very difficult to distract her attention.

She banged her head in the bath-water, seemed surprised that it did not feel like the floor and did not repeat it.

Several days later, she banged her head so incessantly on the floor that she had to be kept off the floor.

At fourteen months: She knocked her head violently when isolated in the empty sick-room.

At fifteen months: When put into her bed for a nap against her wishes, she threw herself against the cot bars and banged her whole body as well as her head repeatedly.

When other children took her toys or attacked her, she always banged her head in despair. Sometimes she would compete with another child for the possession of a toy and then suddenly stop and bang her head instead

When showing affection to Christopher, seventeen months, she repeatedly and gently knocked her head against his.

At sixteen months: She threw herself on the floor and banged her head over and over again when not allowed to take another child's toy.

In the garden she threw herself on the grass when thwarted, bent her head towards the earth, but did not touch the grass. A fortnight later, she began on one occasion to bang her head on the grass, but stopped after the first knock, and with head bent, walked on all fours to another place where no grass was growing and there banged her head twice on the ground.

8. Jack, sixteen months, did not acquire the habit of head-knocking, in spite of the example given by several children in his group. But once, when he discovered his own reflected image in a glass door, he first looked behind the door as if to find his double and then, smilingly, bumped heads with his reflection. He did it eight times, with evident pleasure.

9. Rose.

At twenty-one months: She would sometimes kneel down quickly and bang her head violently on the floor without apparent reason.

At twenty-three months: When told not to do something, she turned round, banged her head quickly three times on a small table and then returned peacefully.

When forbidden to pull another child's hair, she threw herself on the floor and banged her head violently four to six times.

When asked to return another child's toy, she obeyed reluctantly but without crying; then she turned round as if looking for something, grasped a small chair with both hands and knocked her head three times violently against it. That done, she peacefully pushed the chair back to its right place and returned with a cheerful face.

Masturbation. — We have so far not observed any increase in baby masturbation under our nursery conditions. Where the second phase of masturbation, two and one-half to five years, is concerned, our observations are still very incomplete. But, apart from certain cases of problem children with excessive and compulsive masturbation, this auto-erotic form of the child's expression seems to keep more within ordinary limits than the more infantile habits of rocking and head-knocking. The reasons for this difference may be various and require further elucidation.

Summary. — Thumb-sucking, rocking and masturbation betray their function as auto-erotic gratifications unmistakably; head-knocking differs from them in important respects. In the case of the former activities, the child's body becomes the object of its search for pleasurable sensations. In the case of head-knocking, the child enacts on its own body its own aggressive and destructive tendencies. It really hurts itself, but, instead of minding, it enjoys or disregards the hurt. Head-knocking shares a number of important characteristics with the auto-erotic pleasures: both absorb the child's whole interest while they last; both are repetitive; and both have a tendency to increase and intensify while they are enacted; both may at times work themselves up towards a climax.

It is rare for the infantile habits of rocking and head-knocking to reach such degrees under family conditions. They are usually observed in rare individual cases; sometimes in abnormal children; and sometimes under conditions of neglect where children are denied all other outlets. But our rockers and head-knockers were normal, well-developed children in every other respect and certainly were given a reasonable amount of outlets. What is responsible for this increase of auto-erotic and "auto-aggressive" manifestations is evidently the fact of institutional life itself.

THE SMALL CHILD'S WISH TO BE APPRECIATED AND ADMIRED. INFANTILE EXHIBITIONISM.

It is counted as a great educational achievement in the Nursery-School when young children learn to play with their toys or handle the educational apparatus for its interest and without claiming continual attention, appreciation or praise from a grown-up. Many modern educational toys are so constructed that success or failure are either excluded altogether (for instance in some of the apparatus for learning to distinguish between sounds, colors, textures, weights, etc.) or are demonstrated unmistakably by the material itself (for instance insets, puzzles, geometric forms). The child in this way is prompted to test its own efforts and to find its own satisfaction in objective achievement.

These educational devices are directed against a powerful natural tendency in the young child, which is firmly rooted in its instinctual end emotional life. The young child, in this primitive stage of its development, like nothing better than to "show off" and, in its intimate life with its parents, gives free rein to this wish, sometimes greatly to the disturbance of other equally important interests. Mothers always complain that their children will not "play by themselves," that they demand attention in spite of having toys, that they interrupt their play with exclamations like "Look what I'm doing!" "Look what I've done!" or that, when several children are in competition with each other, their "Look at me!" becomes a sort of battle-cry. It sometimes seems as if this insistent claim for admiration outweighed by far the child's interest in the occupation itself.

This tendency to show off or, to call it by other names, to boast, to exhibit, expresses itself in the realm of the child's occupations or achievements, but it neither originates in nor restricts itself to this part of the child's life. In the evening, at the time of undressing and bathing, many small children will get into a high mood as soon as they are naked; they will dance about and play all sorts of tricks with great pleasure and complete abandon. This is all the more apparent, the more they are restricted in this respect during day-time. But children do not only enjoy showing their naked bodies, they equally enjoy showing off their dresses, new shoes, a hair-ribbon; they show their bigness. their cleverness, their being good; at other times naughtiness, illness, bodily hurts may become the subject of their demonstrations. There is, in short, nothing in the child's life, which may not at times be used to claim admiration or at least attention.

Every small boy, at some time in his life, proudly exhibits his genitals in front of his mother. Since this is quickly recognized as forbidden, it first vanishes and then reappears, disguised as a demand for help, for attention to a pain or hurt, etc.

This primitive exhibitionism of the child is met and countered by an equally primitive tendency in the mother, which on its side is firmly rooted in the mother-instinct, namely, the tendency to over-estimate the child. To the average mother the child's features and body seem beautiful or at least good-looking, though the child may look plain to an objective observer. The child's advances in bodily development and its achievements in muscular control, though ordinary steps in normal development, are in the parent's eyes surprising accomplishments. Ordinary intellectual progress is magnified and taken as a sign of future brilliance; small talents are praised out of all proportion. This over-estimation of the child, which is the hall-mark of the mother-child relationship, is, on the part of the mother, a narcissistic reaction. The child has begun life as part of her body; so far as her feelings are concerned, it remains just that in the first years of its life. It is therefore judged and treated, not objectively as part of the outer world, but with the tolerance and subjective over-evaluation which we all extend to our own reactions. Mothers react and judge equally subjectively where the child fails to come up to their expectations: with a deep narcissistic hurt, as if they had discovered a defect or suffered disfigurement on their own body.

Because of this state of affairs, the child, under ordinary family conditions, finds in the mother a more or less willing partner for its display of bodily and mental accomplishments, and derives a great deal of satisfaction from this important side of its mother-attachment. But this happy partnership between child and mother is not destined to last. As the child grows older, the mother's attitude changes, often very abruptly, the child's exhibitionistic advances are rebuffed, and nagging and criticism often take the place of the former admiration, which is then shown to a younger member of the family. Consequently the child itself turns against its own wish to show off, represses it or turns it into the opposite. Over-shyness, diffidence, clumsiness, and all sorts of inhibitions may then take the place of former freedom and abandon. However this may be, this early phase of exhibitionistic development leaves its mark in one way or the other for all later life.

It is easy to see that ordinary institutional life offers little scope for the display and satisfaction of these tendencies. The children, as described before, live a community life, not singled out for partnership with one particular grown-up. This does not mean that these children do not try to show off, boast and exhibit as all children do. But, through lack of response, through dissatisfaction and frustration, their infantile exhibitionism takes a different course. Instead of becoming the carrier of attachment to one person, it displays itself indiscriminately in front of every stranger; it may turn towards the playmates; or, where the child cannot enforce attention through positive achievements, it may concentrate on achieving the same end with dissocial behavior, illness and temper tantrums.

Whenever a child forms one of the substitute-mother relationships which we have described, its exhibitionistic tendencies attach themselves firmly to the newly-found loved person. Showing off may then become overwhelming in its force and use every possible opportunity to express itself.

INDISCRIMINATE EXHIBITION.

1. Visitors to all residential war nurseries, ours not excepted, will notice that single children often run up to them and, in spite of their being complete strangers, show off their shoes, their dresses or other articles of clothing. This behavior is only shown by children who are emotionally starved and unattached.

2. Paul, two, came to us as a completely homeless and unattached child. At first he would claim everybody's attention with his only word "hello" and an empty smile with which he greeted friends and strangers alike. At the age of three, he would still show off to everybody minute objects (buttons, little sticks, tiny pieces of material) which he picked up wherever he went. He was not really interested in these objects, they only served to draw attention to himself.

3. Bob, another homeless child, who had never lived with his own mother, went through a period of intense exhibitionism and masturbation at the age of three. He displayed his genitals indiscriminately in front of everybody.

EXHIBITION WITH ARTICLES OF CLOTHING.

4. Rose, seventeen and one-half months, got hold of the coat of one of the small babies. She wrapped it round her neck like a scarf. When the nurse who saw her said: "How pretty!" she walked round the room with it and looked very pleased. From then onwards, she would wrap around her neck whatever clothes or nappies she could get hold of (even wet nappies, if they were within her reach). She would always look at the nurses questioningly and wait for admiration.

When eighteen and one-half months old, she received a new silk dress for a special occasion. As soon as she was dressed in it, she lifted the skirt and walked about like that. When an apron was put on top of it, she alternately lifted the apron and the dress.

She kept the habit of lifting her dress after this occasion. Very often she looked at her naval when she had lifted her skirt. It was never quite clear whether she wanted the nurses to admire her dress or to look at her navel.

5. Freda, two years, when entering the playroom in the morning would run to whatever nurse was present and say: "Frock, pretty, pretty," holding up her skirt and striving hard to get attention, though it was the same dress which she had shown off many times before.

6. Whenever Edith, two, had a new ribbon in her hair, she would walk about self-consciously fingering it. She showed it to her favorite nurse by pointing to it whenever she met her.

7. Whenever Ivy, two years, had a certain red and white dress on (which suits her well and had obviously been admired by the grown-ups), she would keep on lifting up the skirt and saying: "pretty, pretty." She would behave in similar ways with many articles of dress, or toys, or flowers, but never so markedly as with this particular dress.

8. Teddy, two and one-quarter, had a special passion for hats. When he could get hold of his blue beret, he would parade for a long time in it, trying it at various angles and always coming to his favorite nurse for admiration.

EXHIBITIONISM WITHIN THE SUBSTITUTE-
MOTHER RELATIONSHIP.

9. Bessie, two and one-quarter years, behaved similarly towards her favorite nurse. When playing apparently contentedly with her and a group of other children, she sometimes stopped her play suddenly, lifted her dress and said to the nurse: "Look, me got tummy." At least once daily she came to the nurse, cuddled up against her and said in an excited voice: "Look, my shoe, shoe," pointing at her feet, or holding one foot up for inspection. This happened especially when the nurse was busy talking or playing with other children. The display of part of her body was used quite naively to attract attention to herself.

10. Bridget, between the age of two and three, showed off in every conceivable way with shoes, dresses, a new belt, with everything she could do and with all the real or imaginary presents which she claimed her mother to have bought for her. About the age of two years eleven months she especially showed off with hurts. Whenever she met the superintendent of her nursery, she ran to her and showed a place on her arm or leg, saying: "Look at my hurt." As a rule there was nothing to be seen; sometimes there were remnants of former small scratches.

11. Beryl, three to five years, for nearly two years expressed a special attachment to one of the organizers of the nursery by "showing off" to her. She would follow her about on her weekly visits to the Country House, hold on to her hand and give various other signs of affection. But she never asked for anything material, never asked for sweets or presents; she only claimed appreciation and admiration for her belongings. She usually

began with a stereotyped sentence: "Come and see my Sunday frock." She would then lead the organizer along to her closet or drawer, would feverishly pull out her things and display them. The articles she showed were always the same, but this did not in the least detract from her desire to show them or her excitement in doing so. At other times she did not mention her clothes, and minute hurts, usually on the tip of a finger, were displayed instead.

12. Bob, at four and one-half, when he had attached himself passionately to his family-mother, used every opportunity to show her that he was a "big boy" or a "big man." When, for instance, he went downstairs with her, he often stopped before the last three or four steps and said: "Now you watch me how I can jump." When warned that the distance was still too great for him, he said: "You don't know what I can do," insisted on jumping, and hurt himself regularly. This did not prevent him from enacting the same scene on the next occasion.

SHOWING OFF TO PLAYMATES.

13. Bob, four years, was playing with part of the Montessori apparatus all by himself. Shirley, four and one-half, at the other end of the room, was looking at the toys displayed on the shelf. Seeing a box, in which colored beads were sorted, she said: "Alf did this one day, because he was a big boy, didn't he?" Bob heard this, ran to Shirley and asked her in a very excited way: "What did Alf do when he was a big boy?" Shirley pointed at the box containing the beads. Bob took the box saying: "Me big boy too," but he did not begin to

play with them. He changed his mind after a minute, put them back on the shelf and resumed his former work. It was clear that he was not interested in the beads; it was only the desire to be admired by Shirley which had lured him away from his occupation.

14. Martin lived out a phantasy of being a "big man" between the ages of three and three and one-half. He tried to impress his family-mother, as well as his own mother who visited him daily. He insisted on wearing high boots and sometimes refused to take them off when going to bed. He showed off to everybody in a big cowboy hat in which he appeared even at the breakfast table. He showed his strength by pushing and carrying objects far too heavy for him. Added to this was the display of a loud, deep voice, quite unsuited to his childish appearance. Anyone who was not impressed by these displays was told all day long: "Me big man."

He found it impossible to give up being big, even where it was quite unsuitable. One day he was overheard in a conversation with Bob, four and one-half years. Bob said: "When I was small, I was in a pram." Martin torn between the desire to copy Bob and to remain "big," answered: "When I was small, I was a big soldier — and I was in a pram."

TRANSITION FROM INFANTILE EXHIBITIONISM TO SHYNESS.

15. Anne, at six and one-half, demonstrated clearly how the primitive showing off of young children becomes involved and complicated at a later stage. She was especially graceful in her movements and had for this reason been accepted as a pupil in a dancing class. She liked to display to the nurses what new steps she had learned

in her weekly lesson. But as soon as the people, whom she had collected for this purpose, were ready to watch her, she would hide her face, keep everybody waiting and say that she really could not do it. When told that there was no need to, and when everybody had turned their attention elsewhere, she immediately began to dance, but sometimes stopped herself again after the first steps with the same excuse.

This wavering between evident shyness and even more evident exhibitionism is of course well known, even in adult life. In Anne's case it still served the purpose of drawing even more attention to herself.

INFANTILE CURIOSITY.

It is of equal interest to follow another, closely allied, instinctive tendency of the child's: its curiosity.

One of the benefits modern education has derived from analytic child-psychology is a new attitude towards infantile curiosity. Whereas in former times parents and teachers used to frown on the child's attempts to know, to find out, to investigate and to explore, these activities are now understood to be valuable and legitimate activities in every normal childhood. Under the conditions of orthodox teaching-methods children were forced to acquire knowledge in which they had no interest; therefore they remained uncooperative, except when put under pressure. The modern teaching methods of the nursery and infant schools on the other hand make a point of being guided by the child's own, innate curiosity. The modern nursery school provides toys which take the fact of childish curiosity into account. By playing with them, the child can find out what things are made of, how they fit together, what is inside them, how they can be taken apart and put together again, etc. The modern elementary school (see J. C. Hill *The Teacher in Training; Introduction to Geography, History, Mathematics, Science, etc.*, Oxford University Press) succeeds in finding methods which turn all necessary knowledge, including such complicated matters as history and geography, botany and zoology, chemistry, etc., from formal subjects into food for the insatiable curiosity of the young child. Nursery and elementary schools of this kind can therefore be certain of the full and willing co-operation of their children. It is in this respect not a case of the child having to adapt his wishes to those of the grown-up world; these new successes in teaching are due to the grown-up world having for once adapted its methods to the nature of the child.

The position is less happy where cruder, i.e. less sublimated forms of the child's curiosity are concerned. As described before concerning infantile exhibitionism, these instinctive tendencies neither restrict themselves nor originate in the realm of play and occupation. They reach out indiscriminately towards the whole surrounding world and express themselves no less insistently on all the materials and objects which are in no way meant for the child's use. The infant who is given a Russian doll, or ball, or barrel, is interested to open up and open up until it arrives at the smallest specimen of the series, which is hidden in the deepest inside. But the same urge, which prompts the child to accept this toy contentedly, may prompt it to open up and take to pieces whatever it can get hold of: a woman's handbag left in an unguarded place, the contents of a sewing-basket, or an expensive china doll; older children get to work on alarm-clocks, wireless sets or sewing machines with their countless interesting pieces. Such activities are unwelcome and prohibited because they are destructive. In the same manner much of the child's spirit of adventure and discovery is severely restricted by the grown-ups because it is of potential danger to the child's life.

Childish curiosity is still more disturbing and unwelcome on its earlier level where, as sexual curiosity, it is directed straight towards the body and the intimacies of the parents. The young child gives every evidence of wanting to know everything: how father and mother look when they are naked, or in their bath, or in the lavatory, what they do together when they are in bed; what being married means; where children come from; how they are made; what the differences are between boys and girls. Modern-minded and enlightened parents who try to satisfy the child's sexual curiosity with bits of information, are surprised and distressed at the relentlessness with which the child presses forward from question to question until the answers demanded are far beyond what they had meant to give. When the child is simply refused answers, it will spare no trouble to make its own discoveries. Where questioning into these intimate matters is strictly forbidden, the child's natural curiosity will either become dulled or blunted altogether, including those applications of it which are welcome, or curiosity will displace itself with full force on to harmless matters and produce the well-known compulsive and incessant stream of apparently senseless questioning which has always driven parents to despair.

Where parents, without strict restrictions, just fail to provide satisfying answers, the circumstances of the family setting in themselves will supply endless satisfaction for the child's curiosity. The child will closely observe father and mother in their reactions towards each other; the expressions on their faces, odd bits of conversation, noises heard in the night, will serve as the ingredients with the help of which the child builds up its phantasies about the intimacies of the parents. Children can be helped or hindered in the fulfilment of their wishes "to know," but under family conditions they can never be prevented altogether from getting some satisfaction for these desires.

It is recognized that the most "knowing" children are those of the poorest classes where restricted quarters, beds or bedrooms shared, leave no intimacy of the parents undiscovered. Where children have the freedom of the street, their range of discovery and exploring is enormously widened. On higher social levels the children's lives are kept more apart from that of the parents; there is no running of the streets and all the conventions and decencies which have to be observed oppose the child's curiosity with full force. In rich families the observation of servants and their intimate lives often takes the place of the observation of the parents in providing knowledge.

CHILDISH CURIOSITY UNDER INSTITUTIONAL CONDITIONS.

This digression into the various forms in which childish curiosity expresses itself under family conditions is necessary if we want to understand the position in which the child finds itself in a residential home. What is, under residential conditions, the fate of sublimated curiosity which is directed towards toys and learning? What is the fate of the child's pleasure in adventure and discovery? What are the possibilities of satisfying sex curiosity?

Curiosity directed towards toys and learning. — For the average family child whether it can be admitted to a nursery

school or not will decide, whether its "curiosity" can be
directed into useful channels, for the untaught mother of
the poorer classes will probably be unable to procure the
proper toys and be helpless in directing the child's activities.
Residential nurseries on the other hand, if they understand
the need, have excellent opportunities to offer their children
nursery school-life, -toys and -activities. Some of the most
thoughtful nursery experts have found that the ordinary
residential war-nursery, though often handicapped in becoming a real home for the children, can always contain a
good nursery-school and thus at least satisfy one important
desire of the child. It is true that the residential home does
in this respect not offer more than every good day-nursery
school. But it should at least make a special point of not
offering less.

The child's pleasure in adventure and discovery.—Superintendents of evacuated war nurseries have repeatedly described how young children who have never been outside of
London before their evacuation, enjoyed the discovery of
a completely new country-world with all the unaccustomed
pleasures provided by plant and animal life. These excep-
tional circumstances should not lead us to ignore that the
institutional child, even though given some outlets for his
spirit of adventure which it may have lacked at home, is
on the whole segregated, shut off and excluded from most
of the realities of life. It lives in an artificial world, namely,
a community where infants are in the majority and where
all the activities of the day are centered round the children.
It cannot in this way fail to get a distorted picture of life.
It cannot acquire knowledge of the various jobs and trades,
except those which deal with children; it acquires little idea
of money, since it is not taken shopping or sent on errands;

it has little conception where the necessities of life come from, since things are handed out when necessary. The children never see the buying or hear the plans for it discussed. There is in many nurseries, little opportunity to be alone, or without supervision, or to wander freely, even within the confines of the house. All this works towards establishing ignorance of the world and acts directly against the spirit of adventure.

Curiosity directed towards sex and family matters. — There is no other instinctive urge of the child's for which, in institutional life, conditions are further removed from the normal.

The child has ample opportunity to collect knowledge concerning the difference between boys and girls, i.e. to observe the naked bodies of its playmates. Residential nurseries are, with hardly any exceptions, co-educational, and few attempts are made to separate the sexes for purposes of sleeping, undressing or bathing. The routine of habit training in many nurseries is so arranged that, at least the infants, are taken to the lavatory at specified times and in groups. Shame about bodily functions develops later than usual under these conditions. Whatever may be the matter with the body of one child (circumcision, slight malformations, graver deformities) becomes common knowledge. This does not mean that the infants necessarily form correct ideas of either anatomy or the differences between the sexes. Objective observation conflicts with the results of phantasy and imagination. Young children hold their own theories concerning the use of the various parts of the body and the difference between the sexes and its origin. When what they think and what they see does not coincide, their phantasy usually proves stronger than reality.

According to our observations, infants first notice the difference between boys and girls between the ages of one and one-half to two years. In two cases little girls gave obvious signs of distress when noticing a boy's genitals at that age. Children often react to these first observations in a negative way: instead of remarking on the difference in the genitals which they have noticed, they stress the fact that some other parts of their bodies are alike. A special interest in each other's navels and breasts is shown by many of our children between the ages of one and one-half and two years.

1. Babette, fifteen and one-half months, and Christopher, seventeen months, were potted next to each other. Several times Babette lifted Chris's vest and touched his tummy. Chris pushed her away angrily each time and pulled down his vest, until she gave up.

A week later, she and Rex, thirteen months, were both naked on the changing table at bathing time. Babette noticed Rex's breasts. She pointed to them repeatedly and said something in her baby language. She kept looking at the nurse questioningly, "talking" all the time.

A day later, she and Rex were again bathed at the same time. She discovered her own navel and again looked at the nurse and at it alternately for a long time, "talking" with great intensity. For a second she looked searchingly at Rex, but he was already wrapped in his towel and she did not touch him. A second later she had lost interest.

2. Rose discovered her navel when eighteen months old. She lifted her dress many times a day, pointed at her navel, or touched it. This never happened when she was in her cot or play-pen, only when running about the room.

3. Rose, nineteen months, watched Donald, two months, in his bath. She looked at him with a very serious expression, then lifted her frock and looked at her navel. A moment later she put her hands between her legs, which she had never done at any other time.

4. Annette, twenty-two months, stood next to Sam's (eighteen months) cot one evening when he was being undressed. She kept her eyes fixed on him during the undressing, bathing and drying and only walked away when his nappies were on again. From this day on, she always interrupted her play as soon as she realized that it wa᾽ his turn to be bathed. She watched the proceedings and several times tried to handle him. He was at this time the only boy in Annette's room.

5. Jessie, approximately two years, began to show great interest in her body, especially her tummy, patting it, showing herself sometimes, pulling up her frock during play-time with a delighted "Look, me tummy!" This was followed by a period when she compared her own body with her sister's, her mother's and the nurse's. Conversation during dressing or bathing often ran as follows: "Me got tummy. Mummy tummy? Bessie tummy? Ilsa tummy?" "Mummy nose, Jessie nose?" — "Bessie ears, Ilsa ears, Jessie ears?" — This again was followed by a phase when she tried to lift her mother's and other grown-ups' skirt to look for their knickers.

6. Jim, two and one-half years, examined his body while being undressed, and looked at his navel: "Look, big hole here, very big hole." When looking at his chest: "Me got bubble here, more bubble." He was delighted, then went about the room, asking the other children. "You hole? You bubble?" Then to the nurse: "You

bubble? You hole?" He laughed a great deal while doing this and was very excited.

7. Dick, three years eight months, when looking at his chest, suddenly said to the nurse: "Me got two buttons there, you open it?" He then looked at all the other children's "buttons" in the dressing-room, tried to touch and pull them, then returned to the nurse and said sensibly: "The buttons not open, what are they for?"

8. Bob, four years three months, climbed into his bath while the nurse was outside the room, and covered his genitals with his flannel. When she returned, he shouted: "You can't see my tooti now, it's all gone." When asked why, he said: "If you can't see it, perhaps you think I'm Jane."

9. Bobby, seven years, watched the only baby of the country-house with great interest for a while, then turned round and asked: "And who took out all her teeth?" Her toothless gums had evidently impressed him very unfavorably.

This was only one of many remarks made by our older children, which showed that they believed that a girl's body had been damaged in some way.

Such constant opportunity for watching other children stands in sharp contrast with the manner in which institutional infants are cut off from the intimacies of grown-up life. It depends on chance, i.e. on the location of the staff quarters, how complete their ignorance remains in this respect. Conditions in our two residential nurseries for instance are quite different from each other. In the country house the children pay frequent visits to the nearby staff-rooms and often share meals with their nurses in the kitchen. In Netherhall Gardens the staff bedrooms are remote from the children and the babies and small toddlers never see a grown-up sleep and hardly ever at a proper meal. With the bigger toddlers special arrangements were made to have members of the staff share their meals or they would certainly have formed the idea that grown-ups never eat.

The following are some observations from the room of the young toddlers, fourteen to twenty-four months.

10. Every now and then the nurse would change her overall in the room. Whenever she started to undo the buttons, the bigger children came and pointed at the overall. As soon as her dress became visible, the whole group of children gathered around her. They looked at her in amazement, some shouted, some were perfectly silent. As soon as the next overall was safely buttoned over the dress, they went away again.

11. The children suddenly discovered that the nurse had hairpins which could be pulled out. One day they pulled out so many, that her hair came undone. While she did it up again, one child shouted: "Look, look!" The others looked at her with large surprised eyes and remained silent. They tried to get at the hairpins again as soon as she had finished.

12. While in the garden with the children, something went wrong with the nurse's shoe and she took it off to have a look. Sam, twenty-two months, stared at her stocking in bewildered amazement. She immediately put the shoe on again and he calmed down. He went away, saying: "All gone."

Lack of opportunity to watch and to observe such matters is only one element in a generally abnormal situation. Not only that these infants do not get familiar with all the

processes of grown-ups' dressing and undressing, getting
up and going to bed; they hardly ever see the private
property of adults and — except by accident — have no
opportunity of investigating it; they hardly ever — except
by accident — overhear private conversation. Since parents,
if they appear together at all, only do so for short hours
of the day, the infants can glean no details which pertain
to married life. There is no way of penetrating into the
secret where babies come from, since babies arrive in the
nursery often enough without the elder child ever having
seen their mother. There is certainly no possibility of col-
lecting information about the role of the father, neither in
his relationship towards the mother, nor in his usual role
of protector and supporter of the family.

In the place of an emotionally charged, sometimes very
stormy family atmosphere which stimulates the child's
curiosity, the average institution confronts its inhabitants
with a set routine. It is interesting to see how small children, in the absence of other food for their curiosity, try to
penetrate and investigate the details of such a routine.
The conceptions of "on duty" and "off duty," "off hours,"
the details of medical inspection, become invested with the
emotional significance of leaving or home-coming of parents,
or other family events. Staff-meetings or lecture courses,
the subjects of which remain mysterious to the children,
are regarded by them with jealous suspiciousness as children
regard whatever activities of the parents go on behind
closed doors. Inquiring into the relations of members of
the staff to each other, assumes the importance of prying
into the relations between father and mother.

We are used to seeing children build the picture of their
world after the pattern of the intimacies of family-life

which they have been so eager to uncover; it is somehow with grave misgiving that we see them do the same with the set and artificial routine of institutional existence.

13. As in every nursery, the toilet accessories of our children are marked with pictures instead of with names. The objects of these pictures assume great importance for them. When Nick, three years three months, saw the moon for the first time, he said: "Look, it's little David's moon." For Nick, the symbol on David's tooth-brush and comb did not signify a picture of the real thing; the moon in the sky seemed to him a picture of what was of such importance in the nursery.

14. Susan, at the age of four, first saw the moon one morning from the nursery window. She asked: "Has she been up there all night?" When the nurse said yes, Susan said with great understanding: "I see, night duty."

15. Susan, in particular, concentrated the greatest amount of attention on all the details of rotation of duties. She could be relied upon at any moment of the day to know where anybody in the big concern was busy, who had gone downstairs with a tray for the kitchen or upstairs on some other errand, which nurse had had her off-hours and who was still expecting them, or whose off-day it was. She was not only interested in it, she followed it all with a most critical eye so as to detect any possible flaw in these, to her, highly important ar-rangements.

16. Betty, four years, was a highly sensitive child who entered the nursery in a state of great upset. She had lost her father through death, had been separated from her mother and vaguely knew about the mother's pos-sible re-marriage. She counted the days between her

weekly visits home and lapsed into a bad state when all her calculations were thrown out by a sudden illness of her mother. Her inability to solve the riddles of separation, re-union, death and re-marriage became manifest in a compulsive pre-occupation with "on-" and "off-times." She would ask every nurse, and even visitors: "What is your name? Where do you live? Where do you sleep? Are you off on Sunday? Are you off on Saturday? I am off on Sunday!"

17. Susan, who was ill in the sick-room, was visited by the superintendent of her nursery-department and asked her for a drink. But before the latter had time to do anything, she added, with a triumphant look on her face and in aggressive tones: "In this room you have nothing to decide, you must ask Sister for everything."

18. Conversation overheard between Bertie, five years and three months, and Ray, five years. Bertie: "You know, Alice is the head of the whole house!" Ray: "Yes, but John is the head of the boiler and green-house."

19. A group of children had been moved from Netherhall Gardens to emergency quarters in a staff hostel during the measles infection. When returning to the main nursery was discussed, Anne said: "I don't want to go back to Netherhall. I want to stay in the house where my Ruth lives" (her family-mother). When told that after all she could see Ruth more often in the nursery where the latter worked all day, Anne answered: "It isn't where she works that matters, it's where she sleeps."

20. Katrina, eight years, saw the doctor before the student's anatomy lecture with a big book under her arm. She wanted to open the book, found the picture of a cross-section of a human body and seemed to look at it

with interest and understanding. But before the doctor actually went into the staff-room, she asked her: "And whom are you going to cut open today?" In her imaginings about the goings-on in the closed staff-room, she had turned the theoretical lecture into a horrible operation with one of the students as the doctor's victim.

SUMMARY.

Early instinctive wishes have to be taken seriously, not because their fulfilment or refusal causes momentary happiness or unhappiness; but because they are the moving powers which urge the child's development from primitive self-interest and self-indulgence towards an attachment and consequently towards adaptation to the grown-up world.

To sum up once more:

The infant who shares its bodily pleasures with its mother learns in this way to love an object in the outer world and not merely itself.

Lack of such gratification with consequent increase of *auto-erotic activities* diminishes the child's interest in its surroundings; with excessive thumb-sucking, rocking or masturbation the child creates a comforting world of its own into which it may withdraw and thus become unreachable for outside influence.

The child's *abilities,* gifts and talents develop at least partly in the services of the *wish to be admired.* Appreciation which the child receives may, as shown above, lead to further efforts in the same direction. Rebuff and indifference may have the opposite effect.

Infantile curiosity, if at least partially satisfied, drives the child towards imitation of the grown-up world and thus puts vast energies at the disposal of the wish to

learn and to develop. Refusal of all knowledge or of
the opportunity to acquire it may spread to the child's
intellectual interests and set up inhibitions of all kinds.

The normal and healthy growth of the human personality
depends on the circumstances of the child's first attachments and on the fate of the instinctual forces (sex, aggression and their derivatives), which find expression in
these early and all-important relationships.

THE ROLE OF THE FATHER IN THE
RESIDENTIAL NURSERY

IT is taken for granted by all who are familiar with the conditions of residential nursery-life that there is hardly a place for the father in the residential child's real world. Fathers, of course, do appear as visitors, either on occasional Sundays or on leave from the Forces. But whereas visiting mothers behave naturally enough in the Nursery, deal with their children in a variety of ways, examine their bodies, cut or curl their hair, re-arrange their clothes, bath and put them to bed occasionally and, according to their nature, either overwhelm them with sweets or use the short time together for criticism and nagging, fathers are usually inactive, shy and awkward. They feel uncomfortable in this world of women and children, are at a loss in the face of overtures made to them by their children's playmates, and many of them are obviously glad when visiting time is over. There is nothing in their attitude which might remind the child — even remotely — of the position they would hold under normal family conditions: they are neither the providers of material goods nor the last court of appeal in all matters which concern the child. Though lately some residential nurseries have made attempts to reserve at least some "mothers' rights" for visiting mothers, there are to our knowledge hardly any residential homes which create similar opportunities for fathers.

In this as well as in a former publication* we have repeatedly shown what serious consequences the separation
from the mother has for the child's development. But even
though the mother herself is lacking from the residential
child's daily life, her functions are taken over by other
"motherly" people. The child who is not cared for, handled,
fed, bathed, petted and played with by its own mother, is
thus handled and taken care of by others whom it learns
to accept as mother-substitutes. But there is no one who,
to the child's knowledge, takes over the functions which its
own father, owing to absence, illness or death, cannot fulfil.
Impersonal and invisible powers, i.e. the organization, the
committee, the governors, a board, provide the material
means for the child's upbringing and, by their decisions,
determine the child's fate. These powers are beyond the
range of the infant's comprehension and play no part in
its actual life. There is thus no father-substitute who can
fill the place which is left empty by the child's own father.

We may well wonder why this conspicuous fact has not
attracted more attention or created more concern regarding
the normality of the child's upbringing. Where it is a
question of older children, especially boys, one often hears
the opinion expressed that it is hardly possible for mothers
to handle and restrain them without a father's help; with
adolescents of both sexes juvenile courts frequently quote
in their summing up of a case of delinquency the absence
of the father as the determining factor in the child's dissocial development. It is a matter of common knowledge

---

*Young Children in War-Time, George Allen & Unwin Ltd., for the
New Era, 1942; War and Children, International University Press, 1944,
New York, N. Y.

that one cause of the delinquency of adolescents and pre-adolescents in war and post-war periods is the incompleteness of the family-setting owing to the father's absence in the Forces. But where infants are concerned, the need for the mother and the mother's importance for the child's well-being and physical and moral development looms infinitely larger. The evacuated infants for instance cried above all for their mothers. Retrograde steps in development, as for instance bed-wetting, emotional upheavals, loss of functions and abilities, as for instance of speech, were invariably ascribed to separation from the mother, not the father. Mothers who visit without the father are always welcome; fathers who visit unexpectedly often (perhaps owing to a mother's illness) are often rejected and are unable to bring comfort to the child. When an infant in a residential nursery is confronted by sudden danger (painful medical treatment, inoculation, vaccination), it always calls out for its absent mother. We have never under these circumstances heard a child demand the presence of its father, though in air-raids they will sometimes cry out for their fathers. These and similar facts are apt to create the impression that the presence of the father is of minor importance in the infant's life.

Even if this should be true so far as superficial appearance is concerned (detailed observation of a young child may reveal a very different picture) it is certainly not true in any deeper sense. The infant's emotional relationship to its father begins later in life than that to its mother, but certainly from the second year onward it is an integral part of its emotional life and a necessary ingredient in the complex forces which work towards the formation of its character and its personality.

As described before, the infant's relationship to its mother begins in connection with the satisfaction given to its first needs for nourishment, warmth and comfort. From this primitive starting-point develops the child's love for the mother. The infant normally remains demanding towards its mother though its wishes change from desire for material comfort to desire for love, affection, admiration, knowledge, exclusive possession and all the various gratifications which arise during the successive phases of the infant's instinctual development. The child's love for the mother remains undisturbed whenever she is able to grant satisfaction. When, owing either to circumstances or to her consideration for the child's upbringing, she is forced to refuse satisfaction, the child feels anger against her which, due to the frantic violence of infantile feeling, quickly rises to rage, hate and death-wishes. Normally, the infant after the first two years should be able to tolerate restrictions to a certain degree without violent outbursts: in its further development it has to learn to renounce pleasures willingly for the sake of the mother. This interchange of mother's love for instinctual restriction then becomes the basis of character- and conscience-formation.

The infant's relationship to its father progresses on somewhat different lines. While the acceptance of satisfaction is the main ingredient of the first tie to the mother, the earliest emotions directed towards the father are bound up with feelings of admiration for his superior strength and power. The father in his turn becomes the giver of material advantages and is gradually recognized as the power behind the mother round whom normal family life is centered. But he remains a less familiar figure, removed from the immediacy of the infant's violent reactions by his "bigness" which calls forth in the child the wish to imitate him, to become like him or, in the infant's imagination, to possess his miraculous qualities and exercise them at least in phantasy.

There are two points where disturbances cannot fail to enter into this otherwise satisfying relationship. It is the father's role, even more so than the mother's, to impersonate for the growing infant the restrictive demands inherent in the code of every civilized society. To become a social member of the human community the child has to curb and to transform its sexual and aggressive wishes. What the mother does in this respect in minute-to-minute and day-to-day criticizing, praising and guiding, the father normally re-inforces by his very presence. Though he himself is in the eyes of the child the embodiment of every sexual and aggressive power, his influence at the same time acts strongly in the direction of repression and transformation of instinctive wishes. As in the case of denial from the mother, the child's secret anger and rage is raised against the father by his attitude. The second disturbing element is of, at least, equal intensity. The father of the normal family, who is the object of the child's love, is at the same time the rival in, at least the boy's, fight for the sole attention and possession of the mother. Though father and infant may be the best friends at certain moments, at others they are certainly enemies and competitors where the mother is concerned. The infant bitterly resents its own inferior strength and helplessness in the unequal struggle. This constellation causes hostility and secret revolt against the father, but simultaneously reinforces the young child's wish to imitate and to identify with him and thus to acquire the power to win and possess the mother.

The boy's progress towards adaptation to the grown-up world thus leads through stormy phases of his emotional relationship to the father figure. The possibilities of abnormal development (dissocial, neurotic, perverted) are various: admiration for the father's strength may develop into phantastic fears of the fate the boy might suffer at his hands if he remains either too aggressive or too self-indulgent (masturbation-fears) or too insistent in his wishes towards the mother. Anxieties of this kind may lead to complete giving up of all such desires with consequent passivity, loss of capability, phobias, and inhibitions in all directions. Early and complete revolt against the father, on the other hand, which is not kept in bounds and neutralized by the normal loving side of the relationship, may lead to an estrangement from or break with all the moral demands of which the father was the representative, and thus to the commonest form of dissocial and delinquent development.

Girls, naturally, are spared the conflict of feeling which arises out of the rivalry with the father. They go through a similar phase of admiring love for him which, with them, reaches its climax in the wish to be like the mother and supersede her in the father's affection. The longings and disappointments which arise from this eternally unfulfilled wish fill the child's phantasies, direct its imaginative play and determine its later self-assurance or lack of confidence in being loved.

Far from being of minor importance, the father, where he is present, is thus one of the main determining influences in the child's life. It is worth investigating what happens in those cases where the father is absent and where no substitute figure exercises a similar influence.

RELATIONSHIP TO DEAD FATHERS.

For our resident children it seemed comparatively easy on leaving home to accept the separation from their fathers, and even their fathers' leaving England for services overseas. In striking contrast to this comparative indifference was their complete inability to accept the fact of the father's death where this occurred. All our orphaned children talk about their dead fathers as if they were alive or, when they have grasped the fact of death, try to deny it in the form of phantasies about re-birth or return from heaven. In some cases this happens under the direct influence of mothers who hide the truth from the child to spare it pain; in other cases phantasies of an identical nature are the child's spontaneous production.

1. Susan, four and one-half, who lost her father in the raids: "My father is deaded, he has gone far away to Scotland; he will come back, much later when I am quite big."

"My father is in the Army now. Mummy says he isn't dead any more. The Army is far away."

"My Daddy is in the Navy now, he cannot come back, there is too much water."

"My Daddy is coming next Sunday. Yes, yes, he is coming Sunday. You will see, he will bring me the biggest piece of chocolate you have ever seen."

2. Bertie, five and one-half, whose father was killed in the raids:

"Why can't all killed daddies come back and be little babies and come to the mummies again?"

"God can make my Daddies alive, can't he? Why cannot God put people together again if they have been killed and send them down from heaven? I know why because He hasn't got the things together, all the stuff. After the war God will have everything again. We have — to wait until after the war, then God can put people together again."

3. Peter, four, whose father was killed in the raids:

"My Daddy is killed, yes, my sister said so. He cannot come. I want him to come. My Daddy is big, he can do everything."

"I have seen my Daddy in the street. He has a nice uniform. Yes, yes, it was him; Mummy says he will come back."

"My Daddy is taking me to the Zoo to-day. He told me last night; he comes every night and sits on my bed and talks to me."

Visits from these dead fathers are, if anything, mentioned more often than the visits of ordinary living fathers, and the insistence on their coming is all the greater. The changing phantasies about their activities and the presents which they are going to bring are inevitable defenses against the inner feeling of loss and deprivation.

RELATIONSHIP TO AN ABSENT FATHER.

Julia is the example of a child who never lost or changed her longing for her living father during the whole time of her separation from him. For two years, from three and one-half to five and one-half, she was constantly home-sick for him and talked about him in the most admiring tones and in almost abnormal terms of endearment. She called him "a lovely boy" and described his cleverness, his bigness, in glowing terms in all her bed-time talks. When after two years she visited her family, her feelings broke out with such violence that she overrode her parents' objections and induced them to allow her to stay at home in spite of difficult circumstances. Her father was a small tradesman, elderly, morose, rather strict and uncompromising with his large family of unruly children. In her case the purely positive, loving and admiring element in the father-relationship was particularly outstanding.

The same striking difference between the real aspect of a father and the father-image in the child's phantasy was presented in the case of Tony. Tony had only lived with his family up to the age of eighteen months when the war broke out and his father entered the army as a private. After that time he only saw him on his quarterly leaves, for several days together while he still lived with his mother, and for rare visiting hours after the age of two and one-half when his mother went to hospital with tuberculosis and he was billeted with strangers. After the age of three and one-half when in the Nursery, he saw his father two or three times yearly, sometimes for two days, sometimes for a day only. During the periods of his absence the father would send an occasional postcard and once or twice a parcel with a present; sometimes weeks and months passed by without a sign from him. During visits the father was affectionate and friendly with the child, especially after the mother's death, and showed interest in his pleasures. But in spite of sympathy with the boy, he understood little of the complexity of the child's feelings, introduced one young woman to him on one leave as his prospective step-mother and then, on his next leave, appeared newly-married with another young woman and greeted the child with a demand to "kiss his new Mummy."

Out of this meagre, and in many ways disappointing

reality, Tony fashioned the phantasy of a father to whom
he formed the most passionate, loving and admiring relationship. When he was about four years old, his father
was seldom absent from his thoughts. All his interests
centered round him and he mentioned his name continuously
in every conversation. When he picked blackberries, flowers,
leaves, he wanted to keep them all safe for his father.
When a child fell down and cried, he would say (refer-
ring to an accident of his father's): "My Daddy did not
cry when he fell out of the army lorry, did he?" When
he saw a child run, he would say automatically: "My Daddy
can run much faster." When he disliked having his hair
washed he asked: "Does my Daddy cry when his hair is
washed?" When bathed he would say: "My Daddy can
dive in the water." He would eat greens though he disliked them, so as to "get strong like my Daddy." The big
toe was for him "the Daddy toe"; every army lorry on the
road meant for him the lorry of his father's army unit.
Whatever deeds of omnipotence the other children ascribed
to God, Tony ascribed to his father.

After one of the father's visits Tony did his best to keep
his image alive by imitating him. He developed a morning
cough because his father had coughed in the morning. At
breakfast he stirred his cornflakes with his spoon for a
long time, saying: "My Daddy did this when we had
breakfast together. All the children should do it like my
Daddy." His last demand every evening before falling
asleep was "a story about Daddy." His preoccupation with
his father, the constant use of his name and his attention
to his smallest actions is shown most clearly in a letter
which Tony dictated during this period for his American
Foster-Parent:

". . . I tell you about my Daddy, he is always calling me 'son.' He has been here a lot of days. We had breakfast and tea and dinner together. When my Daddy came back with me in the dark, all the trees were dark in the sky and we could not even see them. My Daddy carried me over the bridge. My Daddy's gun was standing in the corner where my Daddy slept, and when it started to rain my Daddy's hair got wet because I had his soldier-cap. When the war is over, but first I must have my birthday, it will be nice in my house with Daddy . . ."

The over-intensity of Tony's loving relationship to his father was all the more striking since it was preceded, six months earlier, by a period of resentment and hostility. When his father, on compassionate leave, came to inform the boy, then three and one-half, of his mother's death, Tony was shy, hung his head and hardly talked. As a reaction to this visit he told a remarkable phantasy to his favorite Sister. He pointed to a particular spot on the road and said: "I came here with my Daddy and my Daddy chucked a big stone at me and I cried and I do not like my Daddy any more and I will never like him again." When questioned he admitted that he had invented the story, but this did not lessen his hostile feelings. He said: "Do write to my Daddy, I don't want him to come here. I don't want to have lunch with him. Somebody else can have my Daddy." At this time too he listened with interest and pleasure to bed-time stories about his father, but always finished up with the same sentence: "I do not like my Daddy any more."

This outburst of negative feeling in Tony was clearly connected with his old and strong attachment to his mother.

He behaved towards his father as if the latter had actually deprived him of his mother, had possibly had a hand in killing her ("chucked a big stone" at her as he did to Tony in his phantasy). Hate is aroused against the father where his presence seems to separate the boy from his mother; left alone without the mother, son and father are the best of friends. Tony's passionate affection for his father became all the greater since it covered up and hid previous feeelings of an opposite nature.

Their relationship remained untroubled by any of the conflicts which usually arise from necessary prohibitions. The father confined himself throughout to the role of friendly visitor and trusted the task of Tony's upbringing completely to the Sister who was the child's chosen mother-substitute. Wherever the father's influence made itself felt in Tony, urging him towards efforts to become manly and courageous — not to cry, to eat greens — these were the result of spontaneous imitation of and identification with the father and not due to any restrictive or corrective actions on the latter's part.

HISTORY OF A PHANTASY-FATHER.*

Another father whose image was constantly alive in his son's mind was Bob's (from two years eight months to four years ten months). According to Bob his father's feet were bigger than anyone else's; he could run "faster than the puffer trains" and "fly like a bird." He "owned a big big car with lots of wheels on it." He had "golden hair and lovely pink eyes" (when another child praised her mother's

*The observations about Bob have been carried out and collected by Dr. Ilse Hellmann.

blue eyes); he had "much longer plaits" than Betty who had the longest in the Nursery. Though Bob's admiration for his father was to all appearances identical with Tony's, there was one striking difference between the circumstances of the two boys where their fathers were concerned. Whereas Tony's father was, though idealized, a real and living person, Bob's father was non-existent and thus purely a product of the child's imagination.

Bob was born illegitimately and had never known his father. His mother had boarded him out soon after birth and up to his entry into the Nursery he had lived in various homes and seen his mother rarely. From then onward she visited him regularly and he grew very loving towards her. Simultaneously he chose a substitute-mother in the Nursery and attached himself passionately to her.

He first mentioned his "Daddy" at two years and eight months, when he cried for him in moments of despair. This was taken to refer to the elderly foster-father of his last billet. These foster-parents visited Bob twice and on both occasions he sat on the man's lap and cried when he left. This "father" was not referred to again after the first two months. Bob's full interest turned towards his mother, who at this period, worked in the neighborhood of the Nursery and visited him daily.

The next mention of a father occurred at three years two months when he announced: "My Mummy and Daddy are coming on Sunday," and related that he had been on walks with both of them. This was believed to refer to a possible man-friend of the mother's and was disbelieved only when his phantasy developed. He told everybody that his Daddy had visited him in the Nursery, which was certainly not true, and had brought him a toy-car, which was in fact the possession of another child. Bob began to be very sensitive whenever he felt himself disbelieved. He asserted over and over again that his Daddy was real and he would sometimes stop in the middle of a game and shout: "Yes, I do have a Daddy!" though no one had at the time disputed it.

For at least three months he gave no further information about his father, merely re-asserting repeatedly that he existed. At three years five months his father-image took a new and definite shape. Bob at this point went through a naughty and destructive phase and found it extremely difficult to stand denials, to curb his greed, and to overcome his excessive and exhibitionistic masturbation. For the sake of his substitute-mother he tried to cope with all these difficulties, but failed over and over again, and had many outbreaks of temper and despair. His father-image at this time combined forces with Bob's forbidden wishes. Whenever he did wrong, he explained: "My Daddy told me to," or "My Daddy likes it." One of the incidents consisted of Bob's inciting other children to throw all their best soft toys into the garden lavatory. He was extremely upset about it afterwards and admitted: "I did it. But my Daddy told me to."

When he was three and one-half an incident brought unexpected and welcome confirmation for his phantasy. His mother brought a man to visit in the Nursery, and introduced him to Bob as an Uncle. Bob made the widest use of this opportunity. He insisted on calling the man Daddy, held his hand, sat on his lap and generally behaved towards this stranger as if he had found an old and long-lost friend. The man had to sit on Bob's bed in the evening until he fell asleep. He never reappeared, but Bob continued to use him as an important piece of evidence to strengthen the claim for his father's existence: "Yes, and I do have a Daddy for real. You remember, he had a mackintosh and came to Wedderburn Road and he sat on my bed."

At three years ten months Bob invented a new figure, modelled after a nine year old boy whom his mother knew and referred to as "big Bobby." "Big Bobby" quickly developed into an "ideal Bob," who could do everything and possessed everything that Bob wished for himself, for instance a car and a bicycle. Bob at this time made a stand against his own fears and passivity. He began to boast, wanted to pull and push things far beyond his strength and always jumped down more steps than he could manage successfully. "Big Bobby" accordingly could jump high, "right up into the sky." Bob at this time made definite efforts "to be good." Big Bobby was accordingly "always good and when he was naughty the other day, he fell over afterwards and broke his leg all to bits." In sharp contrast to the role of his earlier phantasy-father, Big Bobby did not side with Bob's forbidden wishes. Bob would say, crying: "Big Bobby does not like it when me naughty."

At the age of four his father-phantasy once more gave evidence of violently aggressive images within him. Talking about his "family," he explained: "I have got a new Daddy. The Uncle killed my Daddy and my new Daddy came and killed my Uncle." His father, he declared at this time, was dead. He had "fallen out of an aeroplane. He was a bomb and he fell down and he went all to pieces." This was at a time when Bob began to use swear-words and, instead of being affectionate towards his substitute-mother, talked to her in an aggressive way.

A short time later the father-phantasy and the phantasy of Big Bobby finally fused together. The development of Bob's conscience, made under the influence of his substitute-mother, was reflected in the fact that his father never afterwards did anything that could be considered wrong. He became altogether strong, big and beautiful and, in the course of the next month (four and one-half) took over the function of setting rigth whatever seemed to Bob wrong with the world. When Bob saw a house which had been destroyed by bombs, he said: "My Daddy has lots of bombs which don't break houses." When watching the canary's cage being cleaned of the droppings, he said: "My Daddy does not like his birds to do big job all the time; he puts Calcium in their water." When the Nursery's canary died, he said: "My Daddy has lots of dicky-birds which never die."

The phantasy-image of Bob's father followed and reflected in this manner the course of the boy's development: from careless destructiveness to a horror of destruction — "harmless bombs;" from putting toys into the lavatory to an objection to even birds doing "big job;" and from phantasies about killing to the wish for a world where nobody has to die. When Bob was three years old, his "father" was simply the image of a person whom he could love and admire, and show off proudly to other people. At three and one-half years Bob used his father-image to represent his own instinctive wishes; at four years his father, very much like Tony's father, became the embodiment of everything that was big, beautiful, strong and good. At four and one-half the phantasy-father definitely took over the role of the boy's conscience which had developed in the meantime.

THE GROWTH OF THE CHILD'S PERSONALITY
UNDER NURSERY CONDITIONS

Imitation in the Nursery.

Imitation of grown-ups. — With the young child emotional attachment to a grown-up invariably results in developing resemblances to that person. Infants who live with their parents copy them instinctively in countless ways: they reproduce their facial expressions and their gestures, they naturally use the same words, develop the same tastes, and are decisively influenced by whatever fads or abnormalities may be present in the parents: they copy their abilities and occupations whenever possible. So long as the parents are the only emotionally significant people in the child's world, imitation is restricted to the family circle. When the growing child learns to love, to fear and admire people outside the family, the urge to copy reaches out towards these figures. The daily behavior and the imaginative play of children gives ample evidence of the existence of these tendencies.

The residential child without parents, who has made attachments in the Nursery does the same with the people and the behavior patterns in which its feelings have become involved. Rose, for instance, at eighteen months, said "Oh dear, oh dear" as her favorite words and would screw up her face and nod her head in a certain way. Both peculiarities belonged to the nurse who had had sole charge of this delicate child from the age of two and one-half months. Many children of all ages copy the habits of their "family mothers" with regard to handling other children or their dolls. They use the same expressions for purposes of praise or criticism, they imitate the routine activities of washing, scrubbing tables, putting away clothes; they use the same means to comfort a smaller child or to solve disputes. The result of such imitation is at times surprising and seems incongruous in its high degree of professional efficiency. An aggressive and unruly boy of three and one-half, for instance, who desires to sit on a certain chair, will not tear it away from its occupant, but grasp a footstool which he silently offers in exchange. He imitates a method which he has seen in use innumerable times. Boys of four will act as sick-nurse to others or go on "evening duty" in the dormitory, tidy slippers, carry pots and comfort crying children, not because they have feminine leanings and prefer such activities to the exclusion of more manly ones but because the sick-nurse or the night-nurse is their chosen "family-mother."

Imitation of contrasting behaviour patterns. — Children who are attached to their own visiting mother on the one hand and to their "family-mother" in the Nursery on the other, often have considerable difficulties of combining, not only their affections, but the imitations which result from them. Their mothers' methods of dealing with them are in some cases diametrically opposed to the means used in the Nursery. When this happens children will sometimes develop both types of behavior which they use alternately. Susan, four, for instance wavered between her attachment to a very severe real mother and a friendly and understanding "family-mother" in the Nursery. Consequently she wavered in the treatment of her doll. After the mother's visit she would treat the doll very strictly, nag and scold it and punish it for invented misdeeds. When two or three days had passed by without her seeing the mother, she would revert to the methods of the nursery, speak nicely to the doll; encourage and comfort it, until the same cycle began again with the mother's next visit. In a similar manner her speech and the expressions she used would alternate between what she had heard in the Nursery, and the abrupt, half meaning tones of her mother.

Other models for imitation in the Nursery. — Apart from the "family-mothers" the doctor is the most imitated person in the Nursery. This too leads to a pattern of behavior which seems completely out of place at this early stage. To an outsider the children's attitude in this respect might suggest unusual precocity or abnormal hypchondriacal leanings. But the explanation lies simply in the emotional relationship to the doctor which is a mixture of the affection felt for her as a person; the admiration for her medical tools; the belief in her power over all matters of health and sickness; and fear of the pain which she has to inflict when preventive measures like injections, or small surgical actions become necessary. Imitation of the doctor may express itself in "doctor-play" or in the children's behavior, i.e. display of medical knowledge in daily life.

Bridget, two years and three months, saw a dog eat something off the street. She stopped and called across the road: "Not eat it, doggie! Get diahee."

Martin, three, visited an aunt who gave medicine to her baby. When an hour later the baby was given a piece of cake, Martin shouted excitedly: "Not baby cake, baby diarhea, got medicine."

Janet, four, like all the other children is familiar with the doctor's stethoscope. When she saw the doctor go upstairs with it, she asked: "Somebody coughing up there?"

Anne, six, said excitedly: "You must take Paul's temperature. He never screams, but he is screaming terribly now, so he must be ill."

Summary. — In all the instances quoted, the processes of imitation which are at work in the child are the usual ones. The children copy and take over the modes of behavior which they can watch in their loved grown-ups in the Nursery, just as they would copy their parents and their modes of behavior if they lived at home. If the results of such imitation are unusual or abnormal at times, this is merely due to the unusual and abnormal circumstances under which residential infants are living.

FAMILY BEHAVIOR PATTERNS IN THE NURSERY.

Apart from the types of behavior described above, which are directly traceable to Nursery influence, our resident children develop, surprisingly enough, attitudes which, in normal life are traced back to stimulation by example from the parents.

Infants, between fifteen and twenty-four months, play with each other in either affectionate or crudely bodily ways which, if it happened in the family, would be taken as evidence of their having witnessed affectionate or sexual behavior between their parents. (See *II. Early Relations Between Residential Infants.*) They do so, even though they have never had the normal opportunities of watching their parents or sharing a bedroom with adult people.

Boys, between three and five years, develop the various masculine attributes which are commonly thought to be due to imitation of a father-figure. Where their relationship to their "family-mothers" in the Nursery is concerned, they change at that age from passive dependence and demandingness to manly and protective attitudes. They make offers of marriage, just as boys of that age do to their mothers. Bob Smith, three years eleven months, kissed his family-mother good night, saying: "Good night, Ilsa Smith." Or they offer marriage in the name of their fathers. Tony, four and one-half, shortly after his mother's death said to his favorite Sister: "Couldn't you be my Mummy? Would it not be nice if you would be my Mummy and my Daddy, my Daddy?" They begin to look down on mere females. Bob, four and one-half, asked a young nurse why she was a girl. When she explained that the difference between boys and girls was a natural thing and that people were born that way, he looked at her full of pity, took her face between his hands and kissed her. Instead of demanding protection, they offer comfort. When Tony, four and one half, heard that his favorite Sister had no father and mother, he turned to her and said protectively: "But I am something for you, aren't I?"

This change of attitude happens spontaneously, as a step of development. It may be accompanied, as in the case of Bob and Tony, by phantasies concerning a father; but it is in itself not directly due to a father's influence. Many of these boys have never met their fathers, have never lived in intimate contact with a man or have been separated from their fathers in their earliest babyhood.

Girls, from approximately two years onwards, develop marked motherly attributes in relation to their playmates, to younger children and to dolls, even though they may not have experienced a mother's care from early babyhood nor have had the occasion to watch their mothers with a younger baby. In their case, of course, it is more difficult to separate the pattern of behavior offered by their real mothers from that shown by the nurses.

Imaginative play in the residential Nursery is thus not as different from imaginative play in the day-nursery or in the family as one might expect. The children stage all the usual family-games with changing distribution of roles ("You be Daddy," "You be Mummy," "You be Baby") and compete, as usual, for the role of father.

As shown in the examples of the last chapter, *The Role of the Father in the Residential Nursery*, the children make the widest use of every detail of real family life which they can get hold of. Whenever they visit their parents or receive visits, their reactions in imitative behavior and imaginative play are so strong that one is often led to believe that the most exciting incidents must have happened during those visits. In reality, the most insignificant occurrences or actions on the part of their parents are sufficient to give powerful stimulation to tendencies which lie ready within them. The emotions of the family setting and the patterns of behavior which belong to them are latent in the children and become manifest on every possible occasion. (See Tony's father stirring the cornflakes; Bob and the man with the mackintosh.) Children who have no parents participate in the experiences of playmates. The minority of our children who go home on visits bring back impressions of family life to the Nursery which are quickly taken up and used by those who lack similar opportunities. One child with a living or visiting father can thus spread the conception of the father-figure with consequent play and behavior through a whole group of fatherless infants.

Whenever infants leave their families to enter a nursery, they have to go through a long and painful period of adaptation. There is nothing in their psychological make up to prepare them for community-life. Whenever, on the other hand, children return to their families or are admitted into new families, they re-assume or acquire the emotions and the behavior appropriate to family-relationships in an extremely short time.

DEVELOPMENT THROUGH IDENTIFICATION.

CHARACTER FORMATION.

Every serious type of education tries to produce a state of mind in the child in which it adapts to the standards of the grown-up world, not because it is continually urged to do so, but because they have become its own.

Infants, for instance, can be trained to become clean in a number of ways: through establishing automatic reflex actions, holding out after meals, etc.; through fear of punishment for "accidents;" or through consistent praise for good results on the pot or lavatory. But no child will remain reliably clean for any length of time, and through changing outward circumstances, until it has made the wish for cleanliness its own and feels the same dislike, or even disgust, for dirty habits which rule the grown-up world round him.

Children may be induced to share their sweets with others. In one of our nursery groups they regularly offer the superintendent a percentage of whatever sweets they receive as presents with the words "for your children;" the superintendents "children" are of course their own friends and playmates, but the expression shows that the gift is made out of consideration for their common "mother." This does not mean that they have acquired generosity or dealt with their selfishness or their greed. They are not "altruistic" or "generous" in the real sense of the word until the moment when they themselves, without any pressure put upon them, cannot bear the disappointment or the longing glances of other children without sharing with them. In dealing with aggressive tendencies, education works towards the point when hurting another ceases to be pleasurable and the opposite feeling, pity, is aroused instead.

In dealing with the infantile sex impulses, most parents will not rest content until the child exchanges its own naive enjoyment in their gratification for whatever evaluation or condemnation of them are prevalent in its immediate surroundings.

Such a complete change of heart is only effected in slow stages. In the beginning of life the child is ruled merely by its own desires. It next learns to renounce gratifications for the sake of the parents. Derrick, three and one-half, said about his family-mother: "If Sara loves me, she can't love me wet." In the next phase it begins to share the parent's valuations. Bridget, two years and three months, when placed on the lavatory after an accident during the last stage of her habit training, said with sudden relief: "No more weewee on the floor. Mummy does not like it, Jean" (her family-mother), "does not like it, Bridget does not like it." The educational task is completed in each particular respect when the child stands firm in its newly acquired attitudes, without further need to invoke the images of the people for whose sake this reversal of all inner values has been undertaken. It has then established within itself a moral centre — conscience, suger-ego — which contains the values, commands and prohibitions which were originally introduced into its life by the parents, and which now regulate its further actions more or less independently from within. The firmness and strength, in some cases the inexorability of these new moral powers in the child depend largely on the strength and depth, and the general fate, of the attachments which give rise to them.

It is at this point that the institutional child is at its gravest disadvantage. An infant in a residential nursery may acquire the rough and ready methods of social adaptation which are induced by the atmosphere of the toddler's room; methods of attack and defence, of giving in and sharing, "swapping," etc.; it may further acquire conventions and behavior patterns in obedience to the nursery-routine and in imitation of its elders. But neither of these processes, though adding to the growth of the child's personality, will lead to the embodiment of moral values which is described above. Identification of this latter kind takes place under one condition only: as the result and residue of emotional attachment to people who are the real and living personifications of the demands which every civilized society upholds for the restriction and transformation of primitive instinctive tendencies. Where love-objects of this kind are missing, the infant is deprived of an all-important opportunity to identify itself with these demands.

Our parentless nursery-children, as shown before, do their utmost to invent their own father- and mother-figures and live in close emotional contact with them in their imagination. But these products of their phantasy, necessary as they are to the child's emotional needs, do not exercise the same parental functions. They are called into life by the infant's longing for the missing love-object, and, as such, satisfy its wishes. They are the personification of inner forces, moving in the child, and as such give evidence of successive stages of development. But they are reflections of the child's conscience, where this is being formed under another person's influence, not the originators of this conscience, as real parents are.

The logical people to play this role in the residential child's life are the grown-ups of the Nursery. Success or failure of education in the residential nursery will therefore depend on the strength of the child's attachments to them. If these relationships are deep and lasting, the residential child will take the usual course of development, form a normal super-ego and become an independent moral and social being. If the grown-ups of the nursery remain remote and impersonal figures, or if, as happens in some nurseries, they change so often that no permanent attachment is effected at all, institutional education will fail in this important respect. The children, through the force of inner circumstances, will then show defects in their character-development, their adaptation to society may remain on a superficial level, and their future be exposed to the danger of all kinds of dissocial development.

CONCLUSIONS

THE continuance or discontinuance of residential nurseries after the war will probably be decided by social and economic needs and not on the basis of psychological requirements. In spite of this it may be helpful to have the psychological circumstances of a residential nursery outlined in one's mind. There are realms in the infant's life where the residential nursery can be helpful by creating, very much on the lines of the nursery school, excellent conditions for development, as health, hygiene, development of skills, early social responses. There are, as described above, other realms, where it is important for residential nurseries to recognize their limitations, as in emotional life, character-development; they will then face, and more effectively fight, the consequences of such limitations.

Readers who are familiar with the concepts of psycho-analytic psychology will realize the special interest which has driven the authors to begin this investigation. Psycho-analysis has, from its beginnings, drawn attention to the overwhelming importance of the first five years of life. During this period primitive instinctive forces are openly at work in the child (infantile sexuality with its ramifications and derivatives; primitive aggression). In the first attachments to the parents, the so-called Oedipus complex, the child brings these forces into play, and through identification with the parents' wishes, super-ego formation turns against them and defeats its own former aims. Infantile instinctive life thus becomes for the greater part repressed and unconscious, i.e. forgotten. Its manifestations vanish from the surface and the growing child begins a new life on the basis of its repressions and defenses.

Since we are used to seeing these developments happen under the influence of the Oedipus complex, i. e. the relationship to the parental figures, it is of great interest to us to investigate what happens when the whole family constellation is completely absent; how the child reacts to the lack of emotional response; how it substitutes for it by phantasy activity; and how the inner forces which control, transform or repress the instincts, will contrive to work under these circumstances.

Residential Nurseries offer excellent opportunities for detailed and unbroken observation of child-development. If these opportunities were made use of widely, much valuable material about the emotional and educational response at these early ages might be collected and applied to the up-bringing of other children who are lucky enough to live under more normal circumstances.

THE END